Dear Gloria,

In gratitude
and honor of
your teaching
and support!

Barb + Port

Mort and Barb have created a wonderful and practical workbook to assist couples in unraveling problems, creating vision and deepening growth and connection over the course of a lifetime. This would be useful for any couple in keeping communications clear and connections deep. Well done!

Victoria Wilson-Jones, M.S., Holistic Counselor, Hypnotherapist, Interfaith Minister, Shamanic Practitioner

"*Building the Relationship You Tuly Want* is for any couple that is choosing to move out of the old model of hierarchical relationship to a new model of conscious partnership. Thank you Mort and Barb for this beautiful playbook."

Mackey McNeill, entrepreneur, prosperity advocate, local foodie, nature lover and devoted Grandmama.

"Mort and Barb really do provide a way to improve your life and relationships in 3 days; and then ways to explore to explore learning and growing for the rest of your life."

John Friedlander, coauthor of *Psychic Psychology, Energy Skills for Life and Relationships*

Building the Relationship You Truly Want is a unique and highly personal guide book for course correction and course maintenance in intimate relationships. Mort and Barb allow us to know them not as relationship gurus but as real people who have struggled with, experimented with, and celebrated the challenges of intimacy over time. Their PEP methods are a useful adjunct to support the energy and health of all who read this book. The annual review and renewal process and the one hour weekly meetings are a gift that all of us in relationships can use. This book delivers on its title.

Dr. George Lester, PsyD, Psychologist

Most of us would not attempt to build a house without a set of blueprints nor intentionally weaken the spark that brings two lovers together, but we may neglect its care. It takes time and effort to blow on the spark for it to become a blazing fire by which we warm ourselves. Marriage is a commitment to that spark recognizing its value as the life force of the union. Barb and Mort share their insights that we may find delight in one another.

Carol E. Parrish-Harra, PhD, Wisdom Teacher

"None of us were born with a PhD in intimacy, communication skills, or cooperative coexistence. To go beyond old coping patterns that keep us stuck in a downward spiral requires personal self-awareness—coupled with the desire to change what isn't working. *Building the Relationship You Truly Want* is a grounded guidebook that rewires our perspective through effective "Personal Energy Practices" paired with first hand examples that we can easily identify with, and apply to our own unique situations.

Barb and Mort Nicholson bring years of energetic training to their professional consulting practices helping countless individuals heal and uncover their belief systems.

The result is 50+ years of marriage that serves as a model of transformation that can be used as a template for nurturing responsible "New Earth" relationships.

Their workbook addresses everyday situations, focusing on all the important issues that we encounter with a significant other. If you do the exercises, they will provide the sacred space you need to reflect, reorder, and redirect the course of your life.

Barb and Mort's open-hearted process provides a well-marked map."

Toby Evans, Spiritual Integrationist, author of *Dead, but Not Gone: Are You Part of the Soul-Bridge to Guide Them Home? Keeper of the Circles: Answering the Call to Wholeness* and *Chakra Labyrinth Cards*.
www.sagebrushexchange.com

Building the
Relationship
You Truly Want

in
Three Days
or Less

Manage Your Personal Energy

Talk About the Things That Matter
Deeply to You

Barb & Mort Nicholson

Barb and Mort Nicholson

barb@nicholsonpep.com

mort@nicholsonpep.com

www.nicholsonpep.com

Softcover ISBN: 978-0-9995933-0-1

Design by Deborah Perdue, Illumination Graphics

www.illuminationgraphics.com

DEDICATION

We dedicate this book to our late daughter,
Amy Kelleen Nicholson

Who loved us as we worked through building our relationship and
while she was in the middle of it.

CONTENTS

FOREWORD

I have known Barb and Mort for approximately fifteen years and was honored to perform their fortieth and fiftieth recommitment ceremonies. They are two of the most loving supportive people I know, not only to each other, but also to everyone in their lives. I know that the work they have done together to create an awesome relationship has done just that, and has allowed each of them to become a person that has great relationships with other people. They love life and it shows.

In this book, Barb and Mort have provided a structure to create and maintain effective unconditional listening skills that will help couples create the relationship they desire. These skills not only create a stronger marriage but allows the couples to create better relationships based on actually listening. The book provides the structure and questions for the individuals to sep- arately answer before they sit down with each other. Then they speak and listen and actually hear what each one of them wants in their marriage and what they feel they are currently receiving. It moves the couple beyond just thinking they know what their partner wants and actually listening to what their partner wants! The structure is simple enough that anyone who is committed to building a better relationship can do it. Barb and Mort have done this over the years, and have both listened with open hearts. It is the reason they moved through this experience.

The Personal Energy Practices (PEP) are wonderful and a great way to focus and center before a couple starts their dialogue. PEPs are a way to focus as they individually start answering questions for themselves and before discussing their answers with each other. I have used the PEPs in my personal life and found them very helpful. My favorite one is the Centering PEP where I call all of myself back to me. I need to center many times during a day or week and this helps me center myself in that moment. Releasing Blocks to Joy is another great one. They are all good and by doing the PEP at the beginning of either answering your own questions or communicating with your partner, the couple takes the opportunity to be present with the other in the moment. They have released outside distractions and can be there for each other. This is important and to me, being present with each other is the entire focus of this book. I highly recommend this process to anyone who wants to have a better more fulfilling relationship and is willing to do the work necessary to create that relationship.

Another gift of this beautiful structure is that a couple actually sits down together and creates written goals for themselves as a couple and for their family and life together. The power of written goals, that you actually check to see if you are achieving, is amazing. Many of us set personal goals and business goals but few couples set goals for themselves as a couple. This is a key element of the structure provided here.

Barb and Mort tackled many hard questions and situations in this book and maybe one of the most difficult is End of Life Planning. Most of us do not want to think about our death or the death of our partner. One of the things I know as a minister is that the greatest gift you can give the ones you leave behind is some idea of what you want for your memorial service and resting place. Having those details available to your loved ones are very helpful because they are difficult decisions to deal with when mourning your passing. This is a great gift that all of us can pass on.

I want to thank Barb and Mort for the willingness to share what they have learned as a couple and how they worked together to create a life that works as individuals and as a couple. This book is laid out in a simple format, that anyone who is willing to do the work, can use to improve their relationship quickly. I see this book becoming an important part of my counseling process with couples, before and after marriage, to either improve their relationship or strengthen an already great one. No matter if you are planning to marry or have been married six months or twenty years, this is a great book to guide you to a more fulfilling marriage and relationship.

Reverend Linda Ketchum, Founding Minister Center for Spiritual Living Greater Cincinnati.

PREFACE

What is this Workbook about? What is the reason we offer it to you? We have an imperfect relationship, although much better than 50 years ago. We offer you a process we developed to improve, even save, our relationship. The process in this Workbook is a lot of work. In some of the subsequent chapters, we will remind you of this fact. We made a felt "poster" that reads "Love is a hellava lot of work!" Hanging off the bottom edge is a further note "And it's worth it."

Building the Relationship We Truly Want, In Three Days or Less? Well, sort of. We spent three days doing an earlier version of what is in this workbook. Of course, we needed to do that review work again after a year, although we took a bit less than three days. As you'll read later, we were motivated to change something from what wasn't working to something that might work. In the second year, we found some changes were working.

We have been blessed with two wonderful editors who asked us the reason we wanted to write this book. We have been writing this workbook, sharing personal stories, and taking up a lot of testing couples' time. We hope couples will consider the possibility of improving their relationship, making it more. Further, we offer this as a way that **actually works**. **For a lifetime**. Finally, we offer it at a low cost to make it accessible to people who may not be able to do this work in seminar form. Our intention is to use the proceeds from this book to first recoup our production costs and then donate the rest to Heartmath and local organizations working to stop domestic violence. We didn't develop the cover ourselves or those graphics inside. See the Acknowledgments section. We recommend the people who helped us.

Welcome aboard. The most important characteristics you will need for completing this work are commitment and persistence. Commitment means we **WILL** have a relationship where we respect, honor, support, pay attention to, be proud of, and love each other. Too often, we make up stories about how it is okay to be drifting from the relationship we truly want.

Persistence to achieve our commitment is what really makes this all work for us. Persistence moves us through times of disappointment in external circumstances and people (including each other), in times of falling out of attraction for each other, money trouble, work trouble, kid trouble, trouble with each other. Oh-h-h-h! We persist when our relationship is just "okay," to seriously look at ways to improve. That includes each of us in this relationship.

We know this process works for us. We do it each year and plan to continue until there is only one of us, here. Could it work for other people? We first wrote what we do for ourselves. We asked a diverse group of couples to test it – a time-intensive request. We distributed a "so how did it go?" questionnaire and a request to meet with us so we could hear their experience in person. We really learned.

A comment on diversity. In testing, we included gay couples as well as straight couples. Just because this works for us, an aging straight couple, did not mean it would be helpful to all.

The comments seemed similar from all testing people. Not a big surprise and reassuring. We have included comments from other people who tested this approach in Part 1.

PART 1
Introduction

OUR STORY

 Mort says *"We saved our marriage!"*

Barb says *"We worked and worked to continue deepening our understanding of one another. It has added richness to our lives!"*

About forty years ago, we were experiencing many life challenges. Within the span of a few years, we faced illness, the death of a premature baby in 1974, and an international relocation to Belgium for Mort's job. Stresses that seemed typical for many young couples – adjusting to a new job, finding a home, parenting a three-year-old, house-breaking a new puppy – were amplified by grief, illness, and the pressure to learn a new language and culture. We quickly found ourselves sinking into depression, unable to cope with so many changes all at once. We suspected there were even more challenges in store for us.

For a time, we sought solace in alcohol. We searched for an English-speaking counselor without success. We knew we had a

3

choice. We could give up. We could drift apart, perhaps slowly, perhaps suddenly. Or we could work as a team to resolve our challenges and improve our relationship.

We both agreed; in no way did we want our relationship to be over. We decided we really wanted to work on our marriage.

Both of us joined support groups for expatriates. Barb determined she needed to work, which was impossible in Belgium without Belgian citizenship. We decided she would return to the U.S. to go to graduate school in 1977. Mort supported this decision by requesting a transfer, and even received a promotion in the process! Additionally, Mort took on the role of primary parent while Barb was in school in another city. It felt like a separation. We remained highly stressed due to so many changes. We continued our use of alcohol, but we also both entered therapy.

Our minister loaned us a set of audio tapes related to intimacy. We listened to them in the evening after putting our daughter to bed, both of us snuggled on the couch in the den, under an afghan. The audio tape included exercises we were meant to complete together. "Tell your partner something you have been lying about, or simply just not telling the truth about," the narrator instructed in a soothing voice. Barb looked at Mort and said, "I haven't been telling the truth about how much your travel for work bothers me. I worry about your health. I feel a little bit like a single parent when you are gone. I want to support you in your goals, so I haven't said anything." Mort told Barb, "I understand that feeling. Now that you are in school, I feel like a single parent. I am lost. I haven't said anything because I support you being in school." In that moment, the two of us realized that we could benefit from talking **with** each other, as opposed to talking **to** and **at** each other.

But we didn't follow through.

Finally, in 1980 after Barb's graduation and return home full time, we both decided to join twelve step programs. Part of the individual work in these programs is to conduct a searching moral inventory. That led us to examine areas of our individual lives we hadn't thought much about.

In 1986, and then again in 1997, we attended two marriage encounter weekends where we practiced sharing and expressing our gratitude for one another. Using these experiences, we started and refined an annual relationship review process. We created it from our own experience of the different aspects of our relationship. We started at the kitchen table discussing a list of topics in 1980, and over time the process has become more organized and thorough. The first review took three days! This review has evolved into our Annual Review & Renewal process. These days, we spend about 6 hours sitting on opposite ends of a soft couch.

In more recent years, we have added one hour weekly meetings— **actually** scheduled in our calendars, so they happen.

This is the journey we took to finally get into a room talking **with** each other, looking at what works and what doesn't, and what we want to do about those things. Over the years, to remain true to ourselves and to our relationship, we created a sacred, special time to review, renew, revitalize, and plan. We began calling this the "Annual Review & Renewal," and every single time, it brought us either back together or closer together. Commitment to the Annual Review & Renewal process enabled us to share, in very non-threatening ways, what was happening within us, to us, and how we were changing.

Not only have we become increasingly clear about what each of us wants from our relationship, we have learned how to meet one another's needs – and our own needs – within our relationship. Often, if we had not completed our Annual Review & Renewal, we could have easily slipped away from one another through the simple act of not paying attention to where we were going!

The Annual Review & Renewal process focuses, in depth, on our relationship. It allows us to examine our strengths, areas to improve, passions, joys, and disappointments. Using a number of discussion subjects, this review is a caring, positive, critical look at what we have done **in the last year only.** We discuss how we feel about what we said we wanted to do, how we did it, how we feel about what we did, what works, and what doesn't. With all this in mind, we create intentional goals for the coming year, in detail. **The Annual Review & Renewal** process is not a dispassionate, clinical review of last year's results. That's no fun, and we wouldn't do it. **It is an energetic, mostly fun, exchange.** It affirms that we believe **we** are in charge of our relationship, not external circumstances or people.

Early in this process, we simply sat down and began to talk. As we became more experienced, we realized we needed to be prepared to talk. We started including Personal Energy Practices (PEPs) in our process to facilitate a nonthreatening, safe environment.

As part of our preparation, we made some agreements. We agreed to think about our commitment and our existing agreements prior to our meeting. We promised to discuss any changes we wanted. We agreed to listen to each other without judgment, and to keep an open mind. We agreed to bring our desire to remain intimate on many levels. Above all, we agreed to do the work that maintaining **our relationship** required. Through this process, we learned that relationships require nurture, support, honesty (even if painful), forgiveness, and willingness to understand one another.

Ten years after our first Annual Review & Renewal meeting, we were operating as a team, talking about how we felt, and how we were doing with the agreements we had made. By 1999, we were discussing how each discussion subject nurtured us, both individually and as a couple. Since we use this process to help us have an ever-improving relationship, we **adjust the process** to allow what we do together to actually help us. You can, too!

We have continued to complete our Annual Review and Renewal process, despite the time and energy commitment, since 1980.

We began, occasionally, to hold recommitment ceremonies to restate, often in new words, our commitment to our relationship. As we become different from the people who made the last commitment, we commit again to the new ones we've become. Over 50 some years, we have committed to each other four times. These celebrations were roughly on the occasion of our 20th, 25th, 40th, and 50th marriage anniversaries. In each case, we recommitted to the person we saw in front of us, rather than the person from the past.

After a while, we started hearing two sorts of comments from other couples:

> *"We watch how well you work together, being such different personalities, and wonder how you do it."*

> *"We have adopted you as one of our models to watch and learn from."*

Such comments, when we first started hearing them, were both humbling and exciting. We didn't think of ourselves as models then. In fact, we still don't. But we realized we had developed a solid process that could work for any relationship, and in 2009, we began sharing the Annual Review & Renewal process with other couples. The process worked for them too, even though each journey to talking **with** each other is different. We have mentored several types of relationships using this approach, with good results.

The Purpose of this Book

This Workbook is intended to **help two people help themselves** to a better relationship. We know there are many, many books talking about relationships. This book is limited to any relationship with your "significant other," whether same or opposite sex. We have been blessed with diverse sets of couples using this Workbook as it was being created. It helps all kinds of couples.

This is a "how to do" book, rather than a "read about it" book. Reading and studying any subject is important. **Implementing that knowledge is critical.** We share how we implement our training, studying, and most importantly, our commitment to having a great relationship.

This Workbook provides Personal Energy Practices (PEPs) to help you learn how to manage your own personal energy and the energy that surrounds us. We know we are energy beings. After all, when we no longer have energy, others are left with an inert body and a disposal challenge! Energy in the form of memories, beliefs, feelings and thoughts are flowing through us. Sometimes, these flows disrupt us when we want to concentrate, or be present with another person.

We encourage **you** to first assess your commitment to having a great relationship and, if you are committed, to experiment with the processes we use. Throughout the Workbook, we discuss flexibility—making this process work for you. You can learn more about us and reasons to believe in and experiment with what we suggest by turning to Author Information and by going to the website listed.

What Other People Say
About the Annual Review & Renewal Process

We asked other couples, diverse in various ways, to use this Workbook and to give us information regarding their experience and suggestions for improvement. Here's what they had to say:

"I was very impressed with this Workbook. It was a beautiful process that brought my husband and I closer together and gave us clarity on many issues. My husband and I really benefited from using the Workbook. It did take time and I am so glad that we invested that time. It has helped us to clarify our goals and communicate better with each other. I would recommend it to all couples. Sell the book to be accessible to less affluent."
– Tracy Jo Duckworth, Licensed Massage Therapist

"Creates focus, especially for areas not routinely discussed. This is challenging in a good way. Although the questions in each section are well written, I had trouble getting started. Once I caught onto the scope and range of the process, it was easier. Some instruction regarding what to do if we hit a snag or get stuck is needed."
– Sandy Dulaney, BA, Licensed Social Worker

"The PEPs were really helpful, grounding and focusing. Conscious celebrations and goals are great!"
– Faith Lester, BA music education

"I like the order very much. It builds us up as a couple first and I like your personal sharing."
– George Lester, PSY.D

"Congratulations! What a wide-ranging subject to bring under some kind of control, to mold into shape. I found the process helpful and unsettling as well.

Not sure about one block of time to discuss. Sometimes sections were much too intense and feelings generated in one section spilled over into the interactions in the next section. I prefer to let sleeping dogs lie, but I know that can be a rift builder. I found the questions overly detailed, but we added questions in some sections. So maybe not too detailed!"
– Joyce Lieher, BA English

"Important to have a want-to and need-to attitude."
– Dave Small, entrepreneur

"It was nice to really have a focused time where the appreciations come in bulk and you know the other person is really listening. We are appreciative every day, but concentrating our appreciations gives them more impact."
– Elaine Zumeta, MSW

Good process. Presentation is well organized and clear. Beneficial in that it forces you to engage all the issues that come up in a relationship. Overall excellent structure and format. The individual personal statements facilitate the process very well. The example forms are a plus. Covers key areas for me, specifically family issues. We don't tend to celebrate our accomplishments in any particular way. This process helps us to think how to integrate celebrations into our lifestyle."
– Jay Zumeta, PhD, Professor Cincinnati Art Academy (ret.)

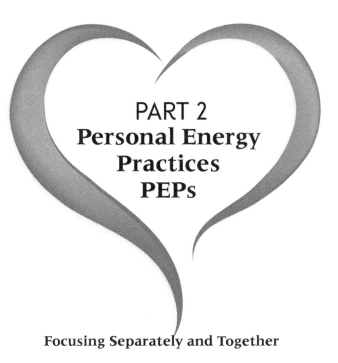

PART 2
Personal Energy Practices PEPs

Focusing Separately and Together

*For Use Before Your Individual Work
and Before Your Mutual Discussions*

PEPs

Personal Energy Practices (PEPs) are a collection of exercises that allow you to experiment with your personal energy. What is personal energy? Our definition, one that we use frequently in our practice as Reiki Masters, is based on the following assumptions:

- Energy is all around us and through us, for example electricity, radio, TV, cell phones, lightning.

- We all have energy, which is **ours.**

- We all have a space around us which we call our own. If someone comes into **our space** uninvited, we may feel uncomfortable, like in elevators.

- We are in communication with people on many levels all the time knowing what someone feels without words.

- We can ask for what we want through our personal energy.

PEPs will help you become quiet and easy with yourself and your partner. They are designed to enable you to review and think about your emotions and discussions from a calm, balanced, and positive center. PEPs keep us focused on our inner energy rather than the external events we all deal with daily. In short, these exercises minimize any additional stresses as you and your partner examine your relationship. We use PEPs daily as a way to maintain our wellbeing, and we have found them to be especially helpful as we prepare for our meetings.

Each Discussion Subject in Part 3 will refer you to one or more of the following PEPs to enable you to experiment and experience that particular subject with more energy and success! This is intended to help each of you to easily move individually into answering the questions. When you meet together, we suggest you again do the PEPs before starting your discussion.

Using PEPs is a suggestion; these discussions will work without doing the PEPs. We find the practices fun and helpful. Some of them we use daily as we begin and end our day. Some are useful during the day as well.

If you have questions about them, please email us at Mort@ NicholsonPEP.com or Barb@NicholsonPEP.com

These PEPs have been developed by us, using materials from John Friedlander[1],[2] Gloria Hemsher, Dennis Drake [3](deceased), and Betty Miller[4][5](retired), all excellent personal energy teachers who have supported us on our way. John and Gloria teach through workshops and individual consultations and have more published books than listed in the footnotes. Visit http://psychic-psychology.org for more information including upcoming training opportunities. You can find many more meditations and PEPs in John and Gloria's books. We selected the sampling of PEPs here to help you have a better life.

---

[1] John Friedlander, Gloria Hemsher, Basic Psychic Development (York Beach, ME: Red Wheel/Weiser Books 1999), 2, 18, 35, 43.
[2] Various training and coaching events with John Friedlander and Gloria Hemsher.
[3] Various training with Dennis Drake, Shaman, 12 Strand Healer, Reiki Master/ Teacher Medical Intuitive/Psychic Healer, Psychic Instructor and Coach, Spiritual Mentor. Deceased
[4] Betty Miller, Licensed Massage Therapist, Tune Up Body Mechanic (self-published 2008)
[5] Various training and coaching events with Betty Miller.

PEP 1:[6]
Balancing & Releasing Other's Energies

Objective: To maintain **your** individual thoughts and feelings.

As Reiki Masters, we have learned to use structured practices to allow energy to flow in and out of our personal energy field. We are all energy beings, each of us surrounded by an energy field, often referred to as our aura. Energy – in the form of memories, beliefs, feelings, and thoughts – flows through us. Sometimes, these flows disrupt us when we want to concentrate. Other times, we consciously direct these flows to improve our lives, through positive thoughts, affirmations, prayer, and visioning.

PRACTICE:

By yourself, close your eyes and imagine another person, such as your partner, parent, boss, or child, about fifty feet away from you. Don't worry about walls. If the other person appears to move toward you, maintain the distance. When you breathe out, allow their energy, stored in you, to flow back to them. When you breathe in, allow your energy, stored in them, to flow back to you. Do this for two or three minutes (or more) until the flow feels easy. When Barb did this, imagining her Mom about fifty feet away, she noticed the energy flow felt like taffy – thick, heavy, and hard to move. She continued for about ten minutes until the flow became easy. She even felt playful and joyful.

Now imagine a large basket between you. When we have connections with another person, we share common memories or pictures. These are like little Velcro patches on us that we can release if we want. So just ask for any sticky places to release from you and drift to the basket. When these feel done, allow the basket to float up into the air and disappear – poof – into gold, sparkly, neutral light, like fireworks. Let it drift off into the Universe for recycling.

---

[6] Based on the work of John Friedlander and Gloria Hemsher

PEP 2: Paraphrasing[7]

Objective: To improve clear communication between you and your partner.

Misunderstandings happen, even when we think we are communicating clearly. A couple we know got into a misunderstanding based upon two simple words. The wife, who was trying to connect to her husband by offering him a foot massage, hit a sore spot. "That's good," he said to her, meaning he wanted her to stop massaging him. She interpreted his statement as "That *feels* good" and applied even more pressure. He jerked his foot away in pain, and said, "That's enough! It hurts! I told you that was enough." Confused, the wife said, "No you didn't. You said it felt good."

PRACTICE:

A simple technique to reduce misunderstanding is to Paraphrase, to say back to the other person what you think you heard. Put what you hear into **your** words. While this technique is especially important when you get confused during a discussion, paraphrasing is important even when you are confident you understand. You may not!

If one partner slightly misunderstands the other, the result is often a response that the first partner again slightly misunderstands, resulting in a spiraling loop of unintentional misunderstanding. We call this the "self-accelerating go-to-hell system." Paraphrasing can reduce the time, negative energy, and frustration that accompany misunderstandings.

Let's start. Take turns making statements, with your partner paraphrasing in their own words, what they think they hear. This can be quite funny and surprising.

---

[7] Based upon training from many sources.

PEP 3: Centering [8]

Objective: To focus your thoughts and become fully present in the here and now.

Center and focus yourself if:
- your thoughts are scattered
- you are thinking about the past or the future to the exclusion of the present moment
- you feel overwhelmed
- you are tired
- you feel stressed
- you are traveling

When we traveled to Turkey from the U.S., we did this PEP approximately every two hours as we traveled. We arrived home feeling good and with minimal jet lag.

PRACTICE:

Relax into a comfortable position. Take three deep breaths. State to yourself:

"I (insert your whole birth name, any childhood nicknames and married names) call all of my multi-dimensional selves to be here now, in this current place and time, and I vibrate in perfect harmony with the energy of the Earth."

People who have changed their names, such as married and remarried women, state all their names in the order they have had them – this allows all parts to be drawn to center. People who have had, or currently have, long term nicknames need to include them as well.

Repeat this 3, 6, or 9 times, until you feel solid, strong, and energized. Enjoy the feeling for a few moments!

---

[8] Based on the work of Dennis R. Drake and Betty Miller

Notice whether you feel totally present in the now moment. If you still are in future or past thinking, repeat this PEP.

If you find yourself "wandering" while answering the questions about your relationships, or anytime in your day, repeat this PEP until you again feel centered. Consider starting your day with this practice.

PEP 4: Grounding [9]

Objective: To attach our energetic selves to something stable

We have learned it is good to be **grounded** – attached to something when we begin to examine our behavior in depth. The earth is the easiest thing to ground to. This PEP allows us to have energy available as we need or want it. Energy is all around us and through us. We may feel tingling or know something is flowing.

PRACTICE:

Sit comfortably and envision, imagine, or feel neutral energy from the center of the earth flowing up through your feet and legs, allowing a pool to gather in your lower abdomen. You may see a particular color, feel tingling or warmth. You may simply know that, with your thoughts, the energy is gathering.

Create a grounding cord, like a tube. Imagine the grounding cord to be about two inches thick, running from the bottom of your abdomen down into the center of the earth. Make it strong and full of life. Allow the pool of earth energy in your abdomen to begin to flow through your grounding cord back to the center of the earth. Encourage the flow to become continuous. This grounds you to the earth.

---

[9] John Friedlander, Gloria Hemsher, Basic Psychic Development (York Beach, ME: Red Wheel/Weiser Books 1999), 2.

PEP 5:
Connecting to Unlimited Energy [10]

Objective: To nourish and energize your energetic self

Practice:

Sit comfortably and envision, imagine, or feel neutral energy from the center of the earth flowing up through your feet and legs, allowing a pool to gather in your lower abdomen. You may see a particular color, feel tingling or warmth. You may simply know that, with your thoughts, the energy is gathering.

Create a grounding cord, like a tube. Imagine the grounding cord to be about two inches thick, running from the bottom of your abdomen down into the center of the earth. Make it strong and full of life. Allow the pool of earth energy in your abdomen to begin to flow through your grounding cord back to the center of the earth. Encourage the flow to become continuous. This grounds you to the earth.

Envision, imagine, or feel soft, golden, neutral energy flowing from the center of the cosmos toward you. Let it flow down the back of your head and down on either side of your spine. There are energy channels there. Follow the flow of energy to the bottom of your spine, and then allow it enter your body. Let it brush over the earth energy, picking up about ten percent of it. Envision, imagine, or feel the energy of the cosmos mixing together with the earth energy, and then allow this mixture to begin to flow up the front of the spine inside your body.

Allow the energy to flow out of the top of your head into a fountain. Be playful; let it take many shapes. Let the energy flow down your face and the front of your body and enter back into your body at your solar plexus just below your rib cage. Feel the energy flow

---

[10] John Friedlander, Gloria Hemsher, Basic Psychic Development (York Beach, ME: Red Wheel/Weiser Books 1999), 18.

to **all** parts of your body. Include your fingers, your toes, your nose. Enjoy the feeling!

Encourage the flow to become continuous by allowing the energy to flow out of your skin, into your energy field and out to the edge of your energy field and back into the universe. Notice the edge of your energy field is about five feet away from you in all directions.

In the next PEP, you will learn to create a boundary to protect your energy flow.

If these energy flows are interrupted, merely repeat the above process to re-ground and re-establish connection to unlimited energy. Interruptions may look or feel like sudden shocks like falling, accidents, or being yelled at. Move to reestablish your connection before addressing these issues. For example, excuse yourself, go to the men's or women's room, sit down, and reconnect to unlimited energy.

Consider starting each day with this process. We both do. Reestablish your connection as needed throughout the day. Remember this process connects you to an unlimited source of healthy energy. Your body will appreciate it!

PEP 6: Keeping Our Own Energy Protected[11]

Objective: To maintain and strengthen your clear energetic boundary

We are beings of energy. So is everyone else. This PEP helps us protect our own energy and keeps us strong.

There are many ways to protect ourselves physically, emotionally, religiously, and spiritually. We may physically or emotionally withdraw. We may pray or meditate. Some people burn sage or take cleansing baths.

PRACTICE:
You can protect your energy with a simple statement, like this:

"I surround my energy field with a colored boundary that allows any energy belonging to someone else to pass away from me, and allows to enter only energy that my higher self knows is for my highest good."

Select any color that calls to you except dark ones, like black, brown, or grey.

Another idea is to remove energy links or cords from you. A cord is an ongoing energetic relationship with another person. It is a source of energy flow. Whether or not you want this flow, it is a drain on your system. First do the boundary PEP above.

State: *"I release all cords connecting me with another. Thank you, it is done, it is done, it is done."* Links return immediately when you think of a person, like your child or your partner, and others. You may have to do this release multiple times to clear links to others that you choose to release.

---

[11] John Friedlander, Gloria Hemsher, Basic Psychic Development (York Beach, ME: Red Wheel/Weiser Books 1999), 54, 113.

PEP 7: Releasing Blocks to Joy [12]

Objective: To let go of language and energy patterns that block our joy

Dr. Albert Ellis developed an approach called Rational Emotive Therapy (RET). He believed that we develop messages that restrict our lives, messages that are expressed as **shoulds, oughts, musts, and have to's**. These messages often appear in our verbal communication when we say things like, "I have to do this" or "I ought to go to see them," or "I should go to the meeting."

"Rule" words, like **should, ought, must** or **have to** may block your joy and may interrupt a healthy relationship. Releasing them opens our lives to new possibilities. In each case, the have to, ought, must, or should, **could** be replaced by "I choose to _____." The latter phrase is much more energizing.

One client discovered that "rule" words expressed themselves very differently in her life. Sometimes they represented things she really wanted to do. She said, "It was easy to change my language when it came to things I wanted to do. I just had a habit of using words like have to and should to express those things. For example, instead of saying, 'I have to go to Zumba tonight,' I started saying, 'I choose to go to Zumba because it is good for my body and lifts my spirits. Those changes were easy to make." What wasn't easy for her was changing the beliefs that came along with "rule" words. "When I lost my job, and no longer could contribute to the household financially, a lot of 'shoulds' started piling up that I wasn't even aware of. 'I should make dinner every night. I should do all the household chores because I'm not working.' These became blocks to my joy."

---

[12] Inspired by John Friedlander in coaching sessions with Mort.

PRACTICE:

To release your blocks to joy, experiment with the following:

Sit comfortably and visualize a bag (your choice – laundry, sparkly gold or garbage). Place the bag in front of you, just outside the edge of your energy field, at least ten feet away. State the following:

"I release all shoulds, oughts, musts, and have to statements from my energy field. Thank you, it is done, it is done, it is done."

Notice what you feel as you say this. You may feel nothing. You may feel a flow, or the sense of a breeze blowing through you. You may notice the bag change shape. If you feel the need for more bags, just visualize more bags. When you have the feeling the releasing is slowing down, allow it to stop.

Then state: *"I release the bag (these bags) to _____."* Fill the blank with the name of an energy that will transmute your released energy, like God, the Universe, etc.

It may or may not be helpful to examine where your **shoulds, oughts, musts and have to's** came from. They may be from others or they may be from yourself, based on searching for how you **ought** to be in the world. Here is the catch: the **ought** for a ten-year-old is different than for a twenty something and so on. We sometimes outgrow the behaviors we learn and forget to release those behaviors. An advantage of this PEP is not needing to identify the source of the rules, merely identify the desire to release them.

You may also wish to thank the **should, oughts, musts,** and **have to's**, if they played a role in helping you cope with life. These "rule" words may represent a method that once worked to help you achieve a goal but now create dysfunction and blocks to joy. For example, one of our clients cut a trip to Mexico short to return for her Grandmother's funeral. "I remember thinking to myself, 'I

should be there.' Even though the word should felt heavy to me, I realized afterward that I truly desired to be at the funeral, not because of any family pressure to be there, but because I needed to be there for myself. I thanked that 'should' for helping me find closure after my grandmother's death, and now I know that I really **chose** to be there."

This technique allows you to release all **shoulds, oughts, musts and have to's** without revisiting them.

Notice how your feeling of joy shifts over time.

PART 3
**The Annual
Review & Renewal
Process**

LOVE IS A

HELLUVA

LOT OF WORK

AND IT'S

WORTH IT!

THE ANNUAL REVIEW
& RENEWAL PROCESS

Welcome to an adventure leading to Joy, Wonder, and Surprise! This Workbook is designed to enable any couple (opposite or same sex) to strengthen and renew their relationship in a positive and constructive way.

Every relationship includes periods of growth in different directions, as well as times of growth in the same direction. The Annual Review & Renewal process will give you a sacred, special time to review, renew, revitalize, and plan.

Just to repeat – What's the Reason We Do This Process?

Mort says because: *"We Saved Our Marriage"*

Barb says because: *"We continue deepening our understanding of one another. This adds richness to our lives!"*

Workbook Structure

The Annual Review & Renewal process covers twenty core topics, which are divided into the Chapters that make up the Parts 3 through 7 of this book. These twenty topics are divided into four domains, or categories, beginning with a focus on you and your partner, and then expanding in increasingly wider circles. The order of the discussion subjects is designed to focus on positive aspects before moving into what may be more challenging topics.

In the first domain – Focusing on the Two of You – you will discover what you appreciate about each other and celebrate your accomplishments. You will explore your communication and decision-making styles and how those styles affect your relationship. You'll assess your feelings about health, intimacy, living spiritually, and time, including who does what around your home.

The second domain – Focusing on Our Immediate Family and Friends – explores topics such as parenting, families, friends, and pets.

The third domain – Focusing on Our World – centers your discussion on the types of activities you are involved in, business and work, finances, holidays and special occasions, vacations and travel, and end of life decisions.

In the final discussion domain – Focusing on Our Future Planning – you will create, together, a vision for the coming year, and set concrete goals that will help you achieve the relationship you both want.

Chapter Structure

Each Workbook chapter follows a set pattern. We begin with an **introduction** to the subject, followed by a short example of **our own experience** with that topic.

Next, we ask you to **"Prep with a PEP"** – referring you to one of the Personal Energy Practices found in Part 2. PEPs will help you become quiet and easy with yourself and your partner. They are designed to enable you to review and think about your emotions and discussions in a calm, balanced, and positive manner.

The next section – called "**Your Unique View**" – includes questions related to that chapter's topic. We developed these questions after years of completing our own Annual Review & Renewal process. The questions are designed to help you understand what is, and what is not, working in your relationship by leading you to understand how the dynamics of that topic impact your relationship, and then helping you to develop ways to create what you want with regard to that topic. Your views of your own choices related to that topic, as well as your partner's choices, are important.

Some of the questions may not apply to you. You may find you need additional topics and/or questions to address matters specific to your relationship. You can choose to use these discussion subjects and/or identify others of importance to you. We suggest first timers use the discussion subjects in the order presented. With experience, the two of you may want to make changes.

Answer the questions separately before coming together for discussions. This order is intended to help you maintain your individual thoughts and feelings. You will individually gain clarity about what you think and feel and, with your notes from this individual time, you can each participate fully in your meeting together. The joint discussion will move more easily because you will come to the discussion with prepared answers. **It is important to take good notes while completing this section.**

Look at **only the last year** for progress, examples, and feelings. If you include more than one year, you and your partner begin to lose details that are important for understanding. Understanding what you want to change is much easier when you see it clearly.

Sometimes, the questions ask you to refer to goals created in the past year. If you are completing the Annual Review & Renewal process for the first time, your goals may be nonexistent for some or all individual topics. In this case, look at your **experience** including your feelings regarding progress, however you define it.

When you have completed the **Your Unique View** section, you will be asked to discuss your answers together. You will be asked to commit to **support** one another as each of you moves to create new ways of being.

Share what you have found during your individual **Your Unique View** time. Share your written answers to the questions or highlight important points. This process is like a treasure hunt! You will find new insights into your relationship. The goal of the discussion is to come to a common view. We have learned we do not necessarily agree; understanding and respecting our partner's view is often enough. Jointly agreeing on a common view or jointly agreeing we have separate views, which we each understand, works for us.

The final section of each chapter is called **Make Your Goals**. Here you will be asked to record specific goals that you and your partner commit to, and what actions you and your partner will take in the coming year to support each other in reaching those goals. We discovered early on that we really needed to record our conclusions and goals. Insights, agreements, intentions, and goals that seem crystal clear in the moment can disappear or turn fuzzy with the passage of time. In a year, you will find your notes helpful. You may want to record some thoughts or discussion points about each conclusion as well. Make note of key items or focus areas. These will vary from year to year. Include items where you concur and where you don't. In the next review, you will know the background. Be sure to include dates. You may even want to post your goals somewhere for easy reference. Our goals list now winds up on the inside of the kitchen cabinet where the coffee is stored.

Keep in mind, with twenty discussion subjects, you can easily become bogged down in goals. **Select high priority goals most likely to move your relationship in important ways**. There will be an opportunity later in the process to refine your goals. There will be more opportunities in future years to further fine-tune or expand upon your goals.

Each Workbook Chapter will refer you to the Discussion Guidelines located below. Review these guidelines before each Discussion until you know them by heart.

After each discussion, summarize your work together electronically or in your notebook. Record notes and agreements from your discussion.

Discussion Guidelines
We have found it useful to follow these guidelines for a productive discussion:

Meet together in a **quiet place** where you won't be interrupted.

Bring the notes you have each made and your notebook (or computer) for recording. You are sharing, rather than exchanging, notes. In other words, use your notes to **talk** rather than handing them to the other to read.

- **Use "I" or "We" statements**, instead of "You" statements. This will keep each of you focused on **your** feelings and examples, as you move from "I" to "We" when completing the worksheets.

- **Listen, without, interruption,** as your partner shares

- Be unconcerned if one of you has more to say than the other for any given topic. Being balanced is unlikely.

- **Avoid blame.** Be willing, open and receptive to one another.

- Remember your shared goal **to improve your relationship**. You have chosen to engage in this process, not to win points or convince your partner to do it your way or be who you want them to be.

- **Remember your manners.** Please and thank you go a long way. Say "thank you" each time after you have listened to your partner.

- **Make note** of any items either of you feel is important.

- Note your goals for each chapter.

Feelings

We often talk about what we "think" about a subject. In the Annual Review & Renewal process, you are asked to think a lot about different discussion subjects. Additionally, you will be asked to notice your feelings or emotions about what you think, conclude, and hear from your partner. Over time, we began to notice more feelings like joy, love, and peace. The following emoticons are intended to give you reminders of feelings you may be having and/or not noticing. Basic feelings include Glad, Mad, Sad, Happy, Scared, and variations.

We like to focus on **uplifting** feelings. Remember that feelings are not "correct" or "incorrect" – they just are. Sharing how we feel with our partner really helps us both understand and move on past the events that we allow to cause those feelings. These emoticons are included to get you started on what will be fun as you create the relationship you want.

Feeling Faces

| Happy | Shy | Romantic | Sad | Scared | Angry |

| Repulsed | Surprised | Shocked | Silly | Teasing | Joy |

Prepare for Your Annual Review & Renewal Process Meeting

Ready to begin? Before turning to Chapter 1 of the workbook, make sure you have done the following:

1. **Root Yourself in Love.** Know, *absolutely*, that you love one another, and that you are undertaking this process to improve your relationship and become closer.

2. **Commit to the Annual Review & Renewal process**. Agree to set aside the time and attention necessary to do the work. Promise each other you will see this process through to the end – no matter what.

3. **Create a dedicated amount of time to yourselves as a couple and mark it in your calendar.** We recommend three uninterrupted days as optimal. If this is impossible, find a way to dedicate several hours to this process over multiple sessions so that you may complete several chapters at a time. Consider whether you want to answer your individual questions on your own prior to the time you set aside for discussion with your partner, or whether you want to include time for your individual reflections as part of this dedicated time. It took us three days the first time we completed this process, but we have also tried separating the days we talk. It can be hard to find three days. We now complete our renewal process in one sitting in one day. Do what works for you.

4. **Decide on a meeting location.** We meet at home in a comfortable room with space to move about. Sometimes, one of us will be pacing while talking. **Managing external interruptions is very important.** As you will see in

the individual discussion subjects, the discussions can become searching and important. While we have done this work away from home, we feel much better doing it in our home. For you, leaving may be needed to find uninterrupted time in a place without distractions. One couple we worked with spent three days on the beach working through the questions.

5. **Decide how you will keep notes**. You may want to purchase a spiral notebook, or you may prefer to keep electronic notes. The Annual Review & Renewal process requires individual reflection and discussion as a couple. Taking notes will help you remember, as a couple, your discoveries, agreements, and goals and will reduce the time you spend rehashing agreements you have already made. We learned the hard way that we would not remember what we agreed to with the specificity needed to make our hopes, dreams, and plans come true. We took few notes in the beginning, which kept us from remembering our agreements, and we often revisited the same feelings and actions the next year. Now we use a student's spiral note book to record our notes. We usually fit about three years of the Annual Review & Renewal process into one notebook. The current spiral note book, with the last three year's work, sits on a bookshelf in the kitchen and is an agenda item once a month in our weekly meeting to review the goals we set for the current year. It is good to remind ourselves of our agreements and how we feel about them.

6. **Make a plan to care for yourselves**. This process may be stressful, particularly the first few times. Care for yourselves. Eat well, drink lots of water, and take time outs.

7. **Plan a Celebration!** The Annual Review & Renewal process is a rewarding process, but it is not an easy or quick one. Plan a reward for yourselves to celebrate your accomplishment. This can be as simple as a shared favorite meal or walk around your neighborhood or park.

PART 4
**Focusing on the
Two of Us**

CHAPTER 1:

Appreciations, Accomplishments, and Celebrations

INTRODUCTION

Start your Annual Review & Renewal process by sharing appreciations, accomplishments, and celebrations. This is a fun place to begin! Spend time listing, and then saying out loud to your partner, what you appreciate about them. This might be a bit new for both of you – both to think about and do. In the day to day business of life, it can become all too easy to forget to appreciate each other. Many times, we have discovered a strength or skill we had not noticed in ourselves until the other said it aloud. Your appreciations are not limited to the qualities of your partner. You might appreciate something you do together. For example, Barb told Mort, "I appreciate our sharing and reading meditations."

With two of you looking at this topic, you'll find lots of things you accomplished – even the little things. As you do this, notice whether you stopped to celebrate your accomplishment at or near the time it occurred.

For example, Barb once said to Mort, "I celebrate planning our trip together." It may seem like a small thing to celebrate planning a trip, but it was an important one to us. Hearing Barb celebrate that accomplishment with her words helped Mort feel recognized for his detail-oriented planning.

OUR EXPERIENCE

Barb

Celebrations and recognition for our growth and change keep us willing to work on our relationship. In the beginning, we were amazed at how well the process worked. It feels wonderful to be understood, accepted and recognized! We had always celebrated socially recognized events like birthdays, anniversaries, and holidays. However, we did this without thinking or sharing much about them. As this process unfolded, we decided to look for the "little" things. As we did, we learned to express appreciations as we went along, as well as during our inventory. This created a change in my consciousness as I began to make an effort to notice and appreciate Mort for doing things like paying bills, making breakfast, asking how I was feeling, or asking if he could help. I love Mort's appreciations of me, like planning and cooking supper, doing laundry or sitting close and snuggling. These helped me feel noticed. We even celebrated things outside our relationship like things we felt good about in our careers.

Mort

Seems like we used to do many things without noticing they were worthy of celebration. Doing but not feeling – that was me! My parents seemed to think results were something to be expected, not celebrated. These days, Barb and I are always finding something to celebrate, like our mutual sixtieth birthday party, square dance class, and cleaning the yard and planting for spring. We also began to incorporate appreciations and celebrations into our weekly meetings.

PREP WITH A PEP

Before answering the questions in this section, consider that the two of you may have been together for some time, long enough to want to improve. Our experience is that your personal energy may be entwined with your partner's personal energy. While this sounds lovely, it is hard to decide exactly what **your** answer is to a question with someone else's energy in your space. We think and respond better when we have only our own energy in our body, and energy field.

Refer to PEP 1: "Balancing & Releasing Other's Energies," Part 2. The benefit of doing this PEP is to release your partner's energy so you can more clearly be aware of your own thoughts and feelings.

YOUR UNIQUE VIEW

Individually, write down your answers to the requests below.

1. Appreciations

The first question will help focus positive energy on your partner.

List appreciations you have for, or about, your partner, over the last year. This may be a long list. You may find more as you think your way through more of the sections in the review process. Appreciations may flow from the celebrations and accomplishments.

2. Accomplishments

The second set of requests is intended for practice in reviewing the past year, as you list accomplishments.

List things accomplished in the last year, as an individual. This is a way to get started, as we often are more aware of what has meaning for ourselves than for others.

List accomplishments *you* noticed your partner did.

List accomplishments *as a couple* in the last year.

Write how you feel about the accomplishments. Note how you feel **now**, rather than how you felt then, about the accomplishments.

3. Celebrations

The third set of requests will help you look at when, how, and why, you choose to celebrate.

List events, in the last year, that you consider being a celebration, like birthday party, promotion party, project completion celebration, and so on. Note how you feel now, rather than how you felt then, about the celebrations.

Which of these did you celebrate with others? Which with your partner? How did you choose how to celebrate? With whom and in what ways?

DISCUSS TOGETHER

Together, repeat PEP 1: "Balancing & Releasing Other's Energies," Part 2, and sitting some distance apart.

Review the "Discussion Guidelines" in Part 3, before sharing.

Begin by sharing your appreciations for the other. Read one appreciation at a time, taking turns. Avoid minimizing your partner's appreciations of you. A response like "Oh, that wasn't much; I would have done it anyway" can have the unintended result of making your partner feel like his or her opinion doesn't matter. Limit your answer to "Thank you." Don't worry if you run out of appreciations first. Being balanced is unlikely. More appreciations will show up as you move through the Annual Review & Renewal process.

You may want to record some of these wonderful appreciations for future reference.

Share your answers for the second question about accomplishments, taking turns. Look at the accomplishments that fostered celebrations and the ones that didn't. Can you determine common reasons for what is celebrated and with whom? What do you learn from that? Could you have celebrated more of the accomplishments? Would you like that as a goal?

Summarize what is important to you both and make note of any items **either** of you think is important, even though the other may not concur. Understanding differences helps you not get in each other's way, even though you don't agree. You may find the differences grow fewer over the years.

As you become more alert to accomplishments and celebrations, you will be excited together. This overall review is an opportunity to look at appreciations you have for the other over a longer period of time.

MAKE YOUR GOALS

Record specific goals that you and your partner agree to commit to, as well as specific actions you and your partner will take in the coming year to support your recognition of appreciations, accomplishments, and celebrations. As a guide, consider the following:

What goals do you want to make individually, and as partners, regarding appreciations, accomplishments, and celebrations?

What appreciations, accomplishments, and celebrations do you want to continue? Which might you want to omit? You may notice some social celebrations are stressful to one or both of you. Make notes.

What do you plan to accomplish next year that could lead to celebrations? What kind of celebration?

CHAPTER 2:
Communication

INTRODUCTION

Communication can be fun and difficult all at once. When we were learning to square dance, we worked to remember names of calls, descriptions, and movements. We communicate differently but ended up laughing about our mistakes. There are many books available regarding the reasons one partner may hear something other than what the other partner intended. We find this often is because we each are different individuals who have had different experiences, which predispose us to seeing the world through different "filters."

A shift in communication can make all the difference. A woman we know who was struggling with her sleep became irritated every time her husband told her, "Sleep soon." He was trying to be supportive, but she felt his words as pressure to evade another night of looming insomnia. "If I could sleep soon, then I wouldn't have a problem, would I?" she answered. Through effective communication, they realized his words were well-intentioned but unproductive. Now he tells her, "Sleep well," a phrase that helps her feel supported. Sometimes one word is enough to shift the communication.

The poem "All I Really Need to Know I Learned in Kindergarten" by Robert Fulghum pretty much summarizes the idea that communication is more than words. The poem reminds us to take care of ourselves and others in a kind, simple and balanced way of looking at life.

All I Really Need to Know I Learned in Kindergarten[13]
By Robert Fulghum

All I really need to know about how to live, what to do and how to be, I learned in kindergarten. Wisdom was not at the top of the graduate school mountain, but there in the sand pile at school.

These are the things I learned:

Share everything.
Play fair.
Don't hit people.
Put things back where you found them.
Clean up your own mess.
Don't take things that aren't yours.
Say you're sorry when you hurt somebody.
Wash your hands before you eat.
Flush.
Warm cookies and cold milk are good for you.
Live a balanced life – learn some and think some and draw and paint and sing and dance and play and work every day some.
Take a nap every afternoon.
When you go out in the world, watch out for traffic, hold hands and stick together.
Be aware of wonder. Remember the little seed in the Styrofoam cup: the roots go down and the plant goes up and nobody really knows how or why, but we are all like that.
Goldfish and hamsters and white mice and even the little seed in the Styrofoam cup – they all die. So do we.
And then remember the Dick-and-Jane books and the first word you learned – the biggest word of all – LOOK.

---

[13] Robert Fulghum, All I Really Need to Know I Learned in Kindergarten (http://www.robertfulghum.com).

Everything you need to know is in there somewhere. The Golden Rule and love and basic sanitation, ecology and politics and equality and sane living. Communication is imperative in **many** ways if we are to understand one another.

Take any one of those items and extrapolate it into sophisticated adult terms and apply it to your family life or your work or government or your world and it holds true and clear and firm. Think what a better world it would be if we all – the whole world – had cookies and milk at about 3 o'clock in the afternoon and then lay down with our blankies for a nap. Or if all governments had as a basic policy to always put things back where they found them and to clean up their own mess.

And it is still true; no matter how old you are, when you go out in the world, it is best to hold hands and stick together.

OUR EXPERIENCE

Barb

Learning to communicate so Mort could hear was quite a challenge! We had to learn from the ground up because we are so different. Our thinking, feelings, approaches, and perceptions are different. It was, and is, sometimes difficult for us. I learned that differences are rich and we could be different and still be in a positive relationship! I learned to say "I want, I need, I think, I feel" instead of "You don't, you never." We had to learn to be a team. Remember those sports cooperation metaphors? We are a team, we cooperate, and we support each other. Also, I found I needed eye contact in order to feel heard or understood. That adds depth and meaning for me. We learned new ways of communicating, and continue to create special meanings as a code, like both wearing purple to indicate our spiritual feelings that day. It's been fun!

Mort

I spent years waiting for Barb to change her behavior (like taking on all responsibilities for doing the housework), thinking all would be well once she did. It never occurred to me that I had a responsibility to state my own needs. The Annual Review & Renewal process has been invaluable for improving our communication because I learned to communicate my needs. Good communication allows us both to feel good. I had to learn that communication meant more than passing information. Learning to talk in a way that strengthens our relationship is a real skill. Also, hugging Barb when she is upset (or even when she is not) sure helps more than anything I can say.

PREP WITH A PEP

Refer to PEP 2, "Paraphrasing," Part 2. Review the "Discussion Guidelines" in Part 3, before sharing. This will help you learn to listen carefully and speak clearly.

YOUR UNIQUE VIEW

Individually, make notes for your answers to the following questions.

1. What do you appreciate about communication with your partner now?

This first question helps you understand what you like and don't like about how you communicate now.

2. How do you feel about the level and quality of your communication over the last year?

Look at both how you communicate with your partner and how your partner communicates with you. Consider both verbal and nonverbal communication.

3. What specific things do you do to communicate, both face to face and electronically?

The second and third questions help you understand how, when, and where you communicate – and how it works. Examples:

> a. Sharing at dinner.
>
> b. Setting a time to talk.
>
> c. Leaving messages to keep the other up to date, like sticky notes
>
> d. Texting
>
> e. Telephone calls

4. Do you keep a calendar? Is it paper, smart phone or other?
Do you share the information with your partner?

5. Have there been incidents arising from gaps in communications?
What were those? List what you remember. How do you feel **now** about both the reasons for the incident and how it was handled?

When you discuss this question, it will give you another perspective; remember to listen for understanding.

6. Do you concur with what you hear your partner says about you?
How do you feel about what you hear? This question helps you look at whether your partner talks you up, down, or not at all, and how that feels.

7. How would you like communication to be?
Different? The same? How, specifically? This question asks you to articulate what you want.

Write down overall feelings, accomplishments, and celebrations for your communication as a couple, over the last year.

DISCUSS TOGETHER

Together, repeat PEP 2: "Paraphrasing," Part 2.

Sometimes discussing how we communicate and miscommunicate can lead toward one or both of the partners becoming defensive rather than listening intently. Be ready to use the paraphrase process from this chapter's PEP as you discuss communication. This will help you better understand what your partner is wanting to communicate. See how this helps cut to the real meaning and stops the "self-accelerating, go-to-hell system."

Review the "Discussion Guidelines" in Part 3, before sharing.

MAKE YOUR GOALS

Record specific goals that you and your partner agree to commit to, as well as specific actions you and your partner will take in the coming year to support your communication. As a guide, consider the following:

What specific goals will you and your partner commit to? What do you plan to continue, add, or change for the coming year? List each.

What actions will you and your partner take, in the coming year to support your communication goals and each other as you achieve them? List them.

Communication is imperative in many ways if we are to understand one another.

CHAPTER 3:
Decision Making

INTRODUCTION

Making decisions easily and quickly requires information and comparisons. Each of you may make decisions differently – in fact, you probably do. Approaching the decision-making process from different perspectives can be frustrating. Articulating – and appreciating – your individual styles of decision-making, and the strengths each style brings to the process, can lead to better decisions. You may consider things you would normally never think about when you choose to decide together!

OUR EXPERIENCE

Barb

When we began this Annual Review & Renewal process, I made decisions looking at what I thought would be the outcome. I also decided based on my feelings or intuition. I think in "big picture" ways. Initially, I felt frustrated by Mort going slow, doing research, and considering what I thought were only "details." For example, when it came to deciding which one of us would manage our money, and how, I just wanted to know if the checkbook balanced. Mort wanted details of where the money went. Boring! After clearly deciding who and how, I began to see value in both ways of thinking. Now our decisions are more mutual. Each of us understands how we got here!

Another example was how we decided to move to the country from suburbia. Mort set up a spreadsheet with decision criteria, things we agreed we needed and wanted. Those criteria decisions were very important to easily making the big decision. Even simple decisions like where to eat out required us to acknowledge and work with our differences. Mort wanted beef, I wanted fish or chicken, and our daughter Kelley was vegetarian, differences which required us to talk together until **we** decided.

 **Mort**
I did not learn decision making skills growing up. This was a real gap. The only process I trusted was to gather lots of data. The truth is I wasn't good at making quick good decisions. After we married, I thought, as the man, I was supposed to make the big decisions, but I found Barb much better at doing that. Talk about a blow to self-esteem! I watched and learned. Even our country house purchase decision was made in two days. The mutually developed criteria helped me feel good about the decision. As we lived together, I learned how to trust my feelings as well as my thinking and became better at quickly making good decisions.

PREP WITH A PEP
As you think about decision making, one key idea is to be centered in the time and place where you are. When we are distracted, it is hard to make good decisions, or do much of anything else. Refer to PEP 3: "Centering," Part 2. This PEP helps you to move away from distracting items (like thinking about the future and past) to be able to focus on the issue at hand.

YOUR UNIQUE VIEW

Individually, make notes for your answers to the following questions. Remember, you are looking for patterns, not the one decision that went wrong.

The first and second questions allow you to look at how you individually make decisions, like you probably did before the relationship, and now as a relationship. People use different resources in different ways.

1. What decisions did we make in the last year?

The ones that occur to you might be big or small. The idea is to have some examples to consider.

2. What do you appreciate about the way you and your partner now make decisions?

The third and fourth questions help you explore these ways. Focus on patterns you and your partner use.

3. How do we make decisions?

Together or separately? Perhaps letting the other partner know later? If our approach varies, in what way and when? Does one lead? Always? Or does the type of decision change leadership?

4. How do we make decisions separately, say at work or in sports?

Question five and six asks whether you might like to change how you make some decisions

5. What resources do you use to make decisions?

Information, feelings, hunches, or other resources? How does your approach vary and based on what?

6. Do you like making decisions on your own? Together as a team? Or prefer your partner make decisions? Which ones?

Question seven asks how comfortable are you with your partner making decisions?

7. How does your partner make decisions?
Same as you or different? In what way? How do your partner's decisions typically turn out?

In questions eight and nine, together reflect on your joint decision making success.

8. Are you comfortable with making decisions together?
What kinds? Are there some you prefer to be involved in making?

9. Do your joint decisions typically turn out well?
If not, what seems to make the difference?

10. Write down overall feelings, accomplishments, and celebrations for your decision making as a couple, over the last year.

DISCUSS TOGETHER
Together, repeat PEP 3: "Centering," Part 2. This will help you better focus on your feelings and wants for your relationship. Sometimes discussing decision making can lead toward the conversation being diverted or, in some cases, one or both of the partners becoming defensive. Staying centered will help with this tendency.
Review the "Discussion Guidelines" in Part 3, before sharing.

MAKE YOUR GOALS
Record specific goals that you and your partner agree to commit to, as well as specific actions you and your partner will take, in

the coming year to support making outstanding, perhaps bold, decisions. These may be jointly agreed actions with one partner taking the lead or deciding what decisions you do together, such as buying something that costs over a certain amount. As a guide, consider the following:

- What will you do the same or differently regarding decision making?
- How will you support each other as you practice your new decision making skills? Perhaps, you will use decision making in areas new to you.

CHAPTER 4:
Health

INTRODUCTION

Health refers to physical, emotional and mental wellbeing. We have heard many times that when you have your health, things are good. Perhaps, you have heard this, too. It seems to come from Grandmother types. Certainly, it seems true for us. We all bring our family genes to the relationship. In our marriage, the good news is we seldom get sick or injured. When one does, the other is available to help. We believe that being as well as possible, given our individual health issues, is critical to our relationship working. We both have chronic health conditions and we support each other in being as healthy and balanced as possible.

OUR EXPERIENCE

Barb

When I was growing up, my parents prioritized preventative care, like doctor checkups and dentist checkups twice a year. They were healthy people who were consciously responsible for themselves. As a result, I grew up knowing I was supposed to take good care of myself. My Dad used folk medicine remedies and chiropractors, so I had a pretty holistic idea about health. I'm blessed with good health. I enjoy learning with Mort about alternative ways to care for ourselves. On a trip to China, we went to a traditional Qui Gong healer and learned how they diagnose using forty-six different pulses! I've always been interested in how to maintain wholeness.

Mort

My Mom was unhealthy and used her illness for attention. I had polio when I was ten; that seemed to turn me from being healthy to being unhealthy. Alcoholism and depression occur in my family. Somehow, I picked up the belief that since I worked in a high stress job, I would have a heart attack by age 55. I did. With my high stress jobs, I was ill, or at least, not well. Working toward behaving in healthy ways and supporting each other in health goals moved me to being well. I get a cold infrequently. Feeling I am not alone with my health problems really helps. Being healthy is even better.

PREP WITH A PEP

Refer to PEP 5: "Connecting to Unlimited Energy," Part 2. This PEP will nurture and support your healthy body. It allows us to have energy available as we need or want it. Energy is all around and through us. As we pay attention to the flow of life, we may feel tingling or know something is flowing through us.

YOUR UNIQUE VIEW

Again, make notes for your answers to the following questions.

The first and second questions ask you to consider both your thoughts and feelings about your, and your partner's, health.

1. What do you think about your health? Your partner's health?

2. What feelings do you have about your health? Your partner's health?

The third and fourth questions open the area of "Is everything okay?"

3. What specific concerns do you have about your own health? Your partner's health?

4. What were your health-related plans or goals last year(weight, diet, exercise, checkups, massages, vitamins, financial contributions to a health-savings account, etc.)?

The fifth and sixth questions allow you to look at your personal health care practices.

5. What current health practices do you plan to continue, add, or change in the coming year?

6. Write down overall feelings, accomplishments, and celebrations for your health as a couple, over the last year.

DISCUSS TOGETHER

Together, repeat PEP 5: "Connecting to Unlimited Energy," Part 2. This will help you stay energized as you discuss a topic that may be scary for one or both of you.

Review the "Discussion Guidelines" in Part 3, before sharing.

MAKE YOUR GOALS

Record specific goals that you and your partner agree to commit to, as well as specific actions you and your partner will take, in the coming year to support your health. As a guide, consider the following:

What individual goals do you have regarding your health in the coming year? Weight, diet, exercise, checkups, massages, vitamins, or other?

What support can your partner give you? What support can you give to your partner?

CHAPTER 5:
Intimacy

INTRODUCTION

Intimacy happens on several levels: physical, emotional, mental, and spiritual. This section will focus on the first two. Refer to the previous chapter on Health, and to Chapter six on Spirituality, to supplement physical and emotional areas.

We've heard people say intimacy is "Into Me, See." Intimacy is about being vulnerable and allowing the other to see who we truly are and what we truly want.

OUR EXPERIENCE

Barb

When we first began this process, we had to separate emotional and sexual intimacy. We kept getting them confused and avoided one or the other. This is not uncommon in the Western culture. Sex is something we do, not something we discuss! I wanted Mort to look deeply into my eyes when communicating and/or during sex. I couldn't say why! It took us awhile to understand and express in a way our partner could understand. Now we understand that each person prefers to be loved in his or her own way. It's my job to remember how, and do that for Mort. I now listen to Mort's details more attentively and support his need to discuss details. He feels supported and close in this way.

Mort

Intimacy means more than sex? Well, that was news to me! I was open to the *idea* of sharing what I thought and believed and felt, but as Barb shared what she thought, felt and believed, I realized I didn't actually know much about what I felt or believed. I could say what I thought, but not what I felt. I learned how to better express feelings and beliefs. In return, she actually listened to me. These years have been exciting, growing, and joyous.

PREP WITH A PEP

Refer to PEP 4: "Grounding," Part 2. This will help you to stay focused on you and your partner now, rather than in the past. It will also help keep any previous partners in the past.

YOUR UNIQUE VIEW

Intimacy has to do with private and personal. Who better to share your intimate thoughts and needs with, than your partner? Most of us are not very experienced at Intimacy in the early days of our relationship. Without focus, this situation can carry on throughout our relationship. This discussion subject is intended to provide practice.

Individually, make notes for your answers to the following questions.

The first question is to help you get clear about what intimacy is, for you, by asking you for your definition. You might want to use an internet search engine to help.

1. What is intimacy to you?

The second question is another one that may be puzzling—look at how feelings affects your intimacy.

2. What do you currently appreciate about the intimacy in your relationship?

The third question builds on the first two. Given what you know, please assess your intimacy.

3. How do you know you are intimate Physically? Sexually? Emotionally? Mentally?

The fourth question suggests there are possibilities available, just for the asking.

4. What do you want Physically? Sexually? Emotionally? Mentally?

The fifth question offers another look at intimacy through helping your partner.

5. How do you support your partner in getting what they want?

6. Write down overall feelings, accomplishments, and celebrations for your intimacy as a couple, over the last year.

DISCUSS TOGETHER

Sometimes, discussing intimacy can lead toward the conversation being diverted. Staying grounded will help avoid this tendency. Together, repeat PEP 4: "Grounding," Part 2. This will help you better focus on your feelings and wants for your relationship.

Review the "Discussion Guidelines" in Part 3, before sharing.

MAKE YOUR GOALS

Record specific goals that you and your partner agree to commit to, as well as specific actions you and your partner will take, in the coming year to support intimacy in your relationship. As a guide, consider the following:

- **What do you plan to continue, add, or change for the coming year?**

- **What specific goals do you have? This may change how you spend your time.**

*Intimacy is about being
vulnerable and allowing
the other to see who
we truly are and what
we truly want.*

CHAPTER 6:
Living Spiritually

INTRODUCTION

In this chapter, we ask you to look at whether living spiritually is part of your individual life and your relationship. This examination can be completed regardless of your religion or faith, if any. The importance of this topic has changed for us over the years. We've gone from very little spiritual focus, to searching for and finding that spiritual values and behavior underpin and support our relationship. Now, sharing our spiritual life is very important to us.

Whether or not you are on the exact same page spiritually is probably not important. We have known many interfaith couples who support each other in living spiritually even though they practice different religions.

OUR EXPERIENCE

Barb
Church was important to my mother, and she convinced my father to participate. I loved Sunday school, singing in children's choir, and even sitting in

church services for Easter and Christmas. Ours was a liberal protestant Christian church, so we studied world religions and toured sacred places of worship for other faiths. I've always been interested in spirituality and have continued exploring new beliefs and practices like meditation. I enjoy exploring my inner world and deepening my conscious awareness. I participate actively in our spiritual center and am a member of Threshold Choir International, which sings at the bedsides of seriously ill patients in hospice care.

Mort

I was raised to go to church and be a "good person." I did notice my parents went to Sunday brunch while I went to Sunday school. No one went to church services. The idea of living a spiritual life went over my head. I was resisting the sin and guilt part and sort of lost it all. Living with Barb was a revelation. For me *being* spiritual, rather than *doing* spiritual, requires attention and focus.

PREP WITH A PEP

Refer to PEP 7: "Releasing Blocks to Joy," Part 2. This will help you release the tendency to view spiritual life from a point of view of rules, e.g. musts, shoulds, oughts, and have to's.

YOUR UNIQUE VIEW

This discussion subject allows you to look at whether living spiritually is part of your individual life and your relationship.

Make notes for your answers to the following questions.

The first question allows you to look at the advantages of your current approach. This may include sleeping in or golf.

1. What do you appreciate about your spiritual life currently?

The second and third questions allow you to look at what living spiritually means to you, from time in the woods to "church" and more. To what extent is spirituality a part of your life?

2. What does spirituality mean to you?

3. Is spirituality important to you?

The fourth and fifth questions allow you to look at what you actually do and develop a basis for new goals.

4. In what ways did you include spiritual orientation and actions into your life in the last year? Examples may include attending a spiritual center of your choice, being in nature, meditation, class work, prayer, reading, or other. How is living spiritually reflected in your behavior and thought?

5. How do you feel about your answers? Star the ideas and activities you will pursue this next year. Are there new ideas?

Write down overall feelings, accomplishments, and celebrations for your spiritual life, if any, as a couple, over the last year.

DISCUSS TOGETHER
Together, repeat PEP 7: "Releasing Blocks to Joy," Part 2. This will help you better focus on your own feeling and wants for yourself and your relationship, separate from what you learned from others.

Review the "Discussion Guidelines" in Part 3, before sharing.

MAKE YOUR GOALS
Record specific goals that you and your partner agree to commit to, as well as specific actions you and your partner will take, in

the coming year to support your spiritual life. As a guide, consider the following:

- **Do you have a common vision for your spiritual life? Do you want one?**

- **How will you share your spiritual life with your partner? Do you want to?**

- **What do you plan to continue, add, or change for the coming year?**

- **What specific goals do you have?**

- **What support will each partner need from the other?**

*Whether or not you are
on the exact same page
spiritually is probably not
important.*

CHAPTER 7:
Time

INTRODUCTION

In this section, you will examine how you choose to spend your most precious resource, your personal time.

This relates to time you use:
- alone
- with each other
- individually with family and friends
- as a couple with family and friends

Achieving a balance in how we use time in our life helps us to have a healthy, happy life as well as a healthy, happy relationship. From time to time, we get out of balance. Our partner can be helpful in letting us know how we are doing; we can receive this information as a gift or as criticism. We can choose.

OUR EXPERIENCE

Barb

Sometimes I felt like Mort didn't like it when I wanted alone time. I felt like I had to "be tough" to get time for myself, even for a simple bubble bath or to listen to music. Finally, we learned to structure our days to include many levels of time, so we could feel better, both alone and together. This is still hard to do sometimes, especially when we are super busy.

 **Mort**
When things aren't going well, I notice I choose to find ways to not be with Barb. With activities and work soaking up big chunks of time, I can fool myself into thinking there is "no time left."
We both pretended spending time together with our friends also filled the need for couple time. As we began to do these annual reviews, we saw our error. We developed goals to balance time alone, alone together as a couple, and together with others.

PREP WITH A PEP
Refer to PEP 4: "Grounding," Part 2. Again, this will help you stay focused in the now. Repeat whenever you feel unsteady or unclear.

YOUR UNIQUE VIEW
Individually, make notes for your answers to the following questions for later joint discussion:

1. How did you choose to spend your time over the last year? Look at a work day and think about how much time was spent, in hours and parts of hours, in each of the major ways. For example, you might consider sleep, personal care, work, time alone, time with family, partner, friends, community, activities, etc. List them by category and time used. Then look at a non-work day. Consider whether this is typical for the last year, or if things changed through the year. Consider time spent traveling separately and together. The idea is to look for information and patterns, rather than a rigorous accounting.

2. How do you feel about your own choices in this division of your time?

3. Thinking about your partner's choices, how does their division of time bring you joy, dissatisfaction, confusion, or other feelings?

4. What do you appreciate about how you spend your time now, individually and as a couple? Seek to understand your partner's choices in your discussion together.

5. How do you each feel about how your partner spends their time and the balance among the various choices? You may or may not agree with your partner's understanding. Seek to understand what may appear to be new information, rather than defend.

6. How do you feel about how you spent your time and the balance among the various choices?

7. Which of the items do you, and your partner, see as choices or see as necessity? This question asks you to consider together which items are options and which items are fixed in place. Consider whether they are fixed because you choose to allow them to be so.

8. Write down overall feelings, accomplishments, and celebrations for your sharing your time as a couple, over the last year.

DISCUSS TOGETHER

Together, repeat PEP 4: "Grounding." Part 2. This will help you better focus on your feelings and wants for your relationship. Staying grounded will help with any tendency to become defensive.

Share your analysis of how you choose to spend workdays and non-work days and how you see each type of day changing throughout the year, if at all. Listen for understanding. Are there surprises?

Review the "Discussion Guidelines" in Part 3, before sharing.

Summarize areas where you both resonate. Make note of any items either of you feel is important. Finally, jointly summarize each partner's choices for how they want to divide their time:

- Time spent at work, including commute.

- Time spent for work in travel, meetings, etc.

- Time spent as a couple without others

- Time spent, as a couple, with your family or friends
    – Your friends
    – Your family
    – In community activities
    – Hobbies, sports, or other activities

- Time spent alone (perhaps in some activity, like reading or other hobby)

- Time spent individually with:
    – Your friends
    – Your family
    – In community activities
    – Sports, or other activities

MAKE YOUR GOALS

Record specific goals that you and your partner agree to commit to, as well as specific actions you and your partner will take, in the coming year to support making good choices in spending your time. As a guide, consider the following:

- **What would you like to remain the same?**

- **What are the areas where you would like to create options for change?**

- **What support does each of you need to make changes in how you divide your time?**

CHAPTER 8:
Personal Responsibilities

INTRODUCTION

Personal responsibilities include or can be defined as who does what around the house, yard, and cars.

This is one area where our models from childhood will show up and may subvert our efforts as we work to have a joyful and harmonious relationship with someone we really like. The idea of negotiating different ways of doing what are fundamentally household chores can be both surprising and annoying. Well done, managing the household will be supportive of a harmonious relationship. Less well done, not so much.

We have both learned that it is easy to prioritize our work over household "stuff." We considered hiring others to do some work, like cleaning the house, as we were financially able. Also, we traded some responsibilities to expand our skills.

Having to do things we don't enjoy can create resentment and become a detriment to our relationship. Doing things together, that neither of us really wants to do, is worth considering. Trading responsibilities from time to time becomes fun.

OUR EXPERIENCE

Barb

I felt super overburdened in the beginning. I had no time to rest or be alone. We would argue when I asked for help. The Annual Review & Renewal process opened a new way to structure household chores. That took the pressure off me and enabled me to relax more.

We hung our "contribution list" where we could see it often, so we remembered what we were to do. That helped, too! We could see how each of us was contributing.

Mort

Early in our marriage, I thought, "Well, if I work and bring in most of the money, why do I have to do anything around home?" With that mindset, I was in for a lifetime of nagging. The good news is Barb is not a nagger. On the other hand, she really felt used, since she was also working and bringing in money. Dividing household chores according to interest and skill really helped us. There are some chores neither really wants. Initially, I always took out the garbage because I was stronger. Now, we have wheeled garbage cans, and we share that chore.

PREP WITH A PEP

Refer to PEP 1: "Balancing & Releasing Other's Energies," Part 2. Also, refer to PEP 7: "Releasing Blocks to Joy." Refer to PEP 4: "Grounding."

When balancing energy, please draw your attention to you and your partner, as well as what needs doing for your home to run smoothly. Then start the Releasing Blocks to Joy PEP to allow any "rules" you have picked up along the way regarding who does household jobs and how they are to be done to move away and be gone. This will allow you to focus on what really needs doing as well as options for getting results.

YOUR UNIQUE VIEW

Individually, make notes for your answers to the following questions.

Prepare a listing of items. There are a number of tasks required to keep a house and a relationship going. Refer to the example listing at the end of this chapter for ideas. To help you, there is blank copy on page 196 as well as the filled-in example in this section. This balance of labor example is for two partners who both work, either outside the home or in the home with growing children. Some of the items on the example may not apply.

The first question is an inventory of what you think happens in your home; your partner may have a different perspective. Sharing your perspectives can help you eliminate the possibility for resentment.

1. Make a list of all the household tasks that need completing on a daily, weekly, monthly, and annual basis. With your list as reference, note how work was divided for the last year. Did it change through the year?

The second question asks how you feel about your contributions, and your partner's contributions.

2. How do you feel about the overall division of labor for the last year?

The third question asks you to look at what is fun or interesting, or at least, not really awful.

3. What do you enjoy? What did you not enjoy?

In the fourth question, you will identify what you and your partner really do not want to do.

4. What do you want someone else to do (not necessarily one of you two)? Is it such an arduous task you need relief? Is there something you would like to learn?

The fifth question asks you to look at what you might want to trade. Remember, this may be a negotiation.

5. What responsibility would you like to change?

6. Write down overall feelings, accomplishments, and celebrations for operating your home, over the last year.

DISCUSS TOGETHER

Together, repeat PEP 1: "Balancing & Releasing Other's Energies," Part 2, and sitting some distance apart. Together, repeat PEP 7: "Releasing Blocks to Joy." Together, repeat PEP 4: "Grounding." These allow you both to become grounded. Allow both your energy and your partner's personal energy to return "home" and allow "rules" about who does what to move away. This will allow you both to focus on what you want and what is best for the relationship.

Review the "Discussion Guidelines" in Part 3, before sharing. Share your responsibility lists. You may each want to have a copy for discussion. If you have different views of who did what, note them and look at them as you work through the list of responsibilities. Add and delete items. Now discuss the first four questions together. Finally, complete a new list for your relationship for the next period of time, a year or whatever you agree to. This will answer question five. Then answer question six.

Summarize areas where you both resonate. Make note of any items either of you feel is important.

MAKE YOUR GOALS

Record specific goals that you and your partner agree to commit to, as well as specific actions you and your partner will take, in the coming year to support your personal responsibilities. Refer to the Partner's Contributions and Responsibilities listing as your goals for the coming period of time. You may want to trade some work items as a way for both to be trained in some items.

These "chores" need doing and you might as well have as much fun as possible.

EXAMPLE

Each Partner's Household Contributions
and Primary Responsibility

Contribution	Barb	Mort	Both	Comments
Regular				*Partner may link to another who actually does the work*
Cards: Paper	X			Birthday, etc.
Cards: Electronic		X		
Cat Feeding	X			
Cooking Breakfast Lunch Dinner	X X X	X	X (Trade) X	Normally Mort
Data Entry Financial Bank Items		X X		
Dry Cleaning	X			
Grocery Shopping			X	
Gift wrapping/ mailing	X			
House cleaning	X			Link to Cleaner
House & Equip Maintenance		X		
Laundry	X			
Litter Boxes		X		
Organizational Filing	X	X	X	Each files own material

Pay Bills with Computer		X	
Pay bills by Hand	X		
Sweeping porches	X		

Watering Plants and lawn
  Inside
  Outside
	X
	X		

Intermittent			
Fertilizing	X		
Financial Review			X
Income Tax		X	
Insurance Claims		X	
Mowing				Neither—condo
Oil Changes		X	
Pruning			X

Spraying
  By house
  Rest of yard and trees
	X		Use hand
			sprayer
			Neither-condo

Travel details		X	
Weeding	X		

PART 5
Focusing on Our Immediate Family & Friends

CHAPTER 9:
Parenting

INTRODUCTION

We learn our parenting skills from older folks: our parents, uncles, aunts, and others. Over the years, we store these skills as memories. These may appear as "should," "ought," "must," and "have to" statements, as well as other rules. Sometimes this results in the idea that we want to parent just like "them" or we want to parent differently from "them." This raises a dilemma regarding what you will choose for your children that really feels good to you. We learned there are many "how to" books with differing points of view. We also learned parenting is a subject where couples often have trouble communicating and working well together.

This relates to time you use:
- alone
- with each other
- individually with family and friends
- as a couple with family and friends

Achieving a balance in how we use time in our life helps us to have a healthy, happy life as well as a healthy, happy relationship.

From time to time, we get out of balance. Our partner can be helpful in letting us know how we are doing; we can receive this information as a gift or as criticism. We can choose.

OUR EXPERIENCE
Barb

As our daughter Kelley began to grow, have new needs, and develop personality and language, Mort and I often had different parenting ideas. These were based on our own experiences with our families of origin. I had strong opinions regarding something being "right" or "wrong." I felt a need to set limits and boundaries, sticking with them when I said "No." Mort was more easily moved to change his mind.

We began to understand that the critical part for us, and our family, was to express love and to **always** operate as a team and not allow children to come between us. Kelley, like all children, was a great little manipulator, and knew exactly how to get us to disagree. **We** had to learn to stand together and parent **together**. We've spent a lot of time on this topic.

Mort

The good news? There were two of us learning to be great parents. The other news? We came from very different family models. Barb's family had a lot of conversation and clear boundaries around behavior. They were kind and thoughtful. In my family, the boundaries were unclear. I basically raised myself, being careful of my father who could go into a rage. I did not care to use him as a parenting model.

We knew we needed help. We even took a course when our

daughter was three. As we became more confident, we expanded our parenting roles to include other children, leading church Sunday programs for high school kids, mentoring at a High School, and adopting an "uncle and aunt" role for our intentional family's children.

Our daughter, Kelley, claimed it would have been better for her to have more rules. Maybe. I do know she was skillful in working us against each other until we started this annual renewal process. I also know she mostly knew how to (and did) make good decisions in personal choices.

PREP WITH A PEP

Refer to PEP 1: "Balancing & Releasing Other's Energies," Part 2. This opens the possibility for each of you to choose your parenting methods. Some of these will probably be what you learned when growing up, some from friends, some from books or classes, and some from experience.

Also, refer to PEP 7: "Releasing Blocks to Joy." We also pick up many "should, ought, must, have to" rules about parenting as we mature. Some rules may limit us choosing how to be the parents we want to be. Consider releasing them.

YOUR UNIQUE VIEW

Jointly agree the children you will "parent." This list might include your own children, nieces, nephews, grandchildren, God children, and children from extended or intentional families. These last two are usually not blood relatives, rather children you want to spend family-style time with and in some significant way feel responsible for. This may be complex, particularly in a blended, extended, large family. You may want to just start with the ones closest to you.

These questions are focused on you and your partner as parents, rather than on the successes of your children. From time to time, parents choose to relive their past successes or avoid past disappointments through their children. Examining your **own** parenting skills will better help everyone move toward their goals.

Individually, make notes for your answers to the following questions.

1. Overall Parenting Experience. Write down overall feelings, accomplishments, and celebrations for your parenting as a couple, over the last year, in general. There may be differences in each of your styles, which you can capture here. This question examines how you feel about parenting, as well as your successes and challenges. Take some time to celebrate.

2. Each Child. What are your **feelings** about the last year as related to your parenting, individually and as a couple, to each child? List each child separately. Be sure you are each considering the same children. This question helps you learn more about how you parent each child.

Specifically, you may have different feelings, accomplishments, and celebrations for different children, grandchildren, god children, nieces, nephews, etc. There may be differences for each of you. Remember to begin with those closest to you.

Notice if there are specific incidents, behaviors, or beliefs related to those feelings? Include them in your list for each child. This will help you to get to know yourself and each child better.

3. Your Accomplishments. What specific accomplishments were you and your partner hoping or expecting for your relationship with your children, in general, and for each child? What did you actually accomplish? Were these expectations shared with the child? You may be surprised at how much you have in common for each child. This question clarifies what work is yours to do (individually, and as a couple), and what work is the child's to do as they learn to be the way they want to be.

4. Write down overall feelings, accomplishments, and celebrations for your parenting as a couple, over the last year.

DISCUSS TOGETHER

Together, repeat PEP 1: "Balancing & Releasing Other's Energies," Part 2, and sitting some distance apart. Together, repeat PEP 7: "Releasing Blocks to Joy." This will help you better focus on your feelings and wants for your relationship, separate from what you learned from others.

Review the "Discussion Guidelines" in Part 3, before sharing. As you listen to your partner, you can learn even more about each child. Summarize areas where you both resonate. Make note of any items either of you feel is important.

MAKE YOUR GOALS

Record specific goals that you and your partner agree to commit to, as well as specific actions you and your partner will take, in the coming year to support excellent parenting. As a guide, consider the following:

- **What will you continue, add, or change in the coming year?**

- **How will you support each child, as they are, at their stage of development?**

- **Which partner will take what role with each child?**

- **What will you do with each child? Help one child develop a specific skill, or spend individual time or couple time with each child?**

- **What will you do with children as a family (for example, travel and holidays)?**

Our partner can be helpful in letting us know how we are doing; we can receive this information as a gift or as criticism. We can choose.

CHAPTER 10:
Our Families
Including Extended & Intentional

INTRODUCTION

We have many definitions of "family." We start with our family of origin, blood-related or adopted, and then move to include:

- **Blended families,** as parents remarry or join new life partners and their families.

- **Extended families,** including people close to us like aunts, uncles, cousins and in laws.

- **Intentional family,** people who are not blood related, but with whom we choose to be close and include in family celebrations.

This section helps you understand each other's relationships with family, how you work with important groups of people, and how you want to build or maintain those relationships in the coming year.

OUR EXPERIENCE

Barb

Because Mort and I came from very different family backgrounds, in the beginning we found it helpful to share how our families handled each topic in this workbook. We gained an in-depth understanding of where we came from. What did we like or not like about our family? What did we want to do differently? What did we want to do the same? These could be values or behavior.

My family hugged, laughed, and talked. Meals were a time to share our day's experience or talk about new learnings, the news, and politics. Our first vacation with Mort's folks driving to California from Nebraska was a revelation! Whenever we stopped to eat in a restaurant, I would be chatting away while they just ate and then got up to leave! Farm families (his anyway) just ate and got back to work!

Mort

Barb's family was a revelation to me – they hugged! Her Mom didn't really like me (at least so I thought). Barb had a similar experience with my family. They didn't hug (although she did anyway). My Mom did like her. When we developed a common view about our families, our life got easier. I like hugging.

When we moved 750 miles away from our families, we realized we were too far to visit more than a couple times a year. Starting in 1968, we found other families in the same situation and created an intentional family. Over the years, this gave us courage to approach our families of origin more often and with better results.

PREP WITH A PEP

You have many "rules" about your families, often stated as "I should," "I have to," "I must," or "I ought to." We all developed these rules over the years and in many different situations. Your partner had this experience as well, and there is a good chance some of the "shoulds," "oughts," "musts," and "have to's" are different for each of you. Refer to PEP 7: "Releasing Blocks to Joy," Part 2.

YOUR UNIQUE VIEW

Jointly agree which families you want to consider. You may want to just start with a single family for each until you get comfortable with this process. Remember, the goal is to improve your relationship and learn how you work with important groups of people.

The following questions focus on you and your partner in relationship to your families, both as a single and as part of your relationship. You and your partner form a new unit. For many families, this new unit will be more or less understood and welcomed within existing family structures. Occasionally, this new unit may not be welcomed at all, particularly when your partnership conflicts with certain values related to sexuality, faith, or ethnicity. Your parents may be glad you have a partner, or they may not. Your relationship is a change for existing family groups, and even though they recognize the change, they may resist it. Regardless of whether your family recognizes or welcomes your partnership, talking about the kind of relationship you want with your families is useful.

Individually, make notes for your answers to the following questions:

The first and second questions give you an opportunity to step back a bit and identify feelings, such as pride, disappointment, confusion, and so on.

1. List your feelings about your family of origin and, then separately, your partner's family of origin, if you know the family. If you were adopted, you may need to consider both biological and adopted families. Consider the family with whom you lived longest as the primary family for this exercise. Depending upon relationships with biological parents, you will need to include both types of family. You may find your attention being drawn to certain individuals. Make notes as to the reasons for this, if you know.

2. One, or both of you, may not have close family ties. If so, how do you feel about that?

The third and fourth questions recognize that we are often far away from our family of origin, and have formed close friends into an "intentional family," the people whom you can call at 3AM if you need to. Since this formation may not have been a planned process, this gives you an opportunity to look at how you feel about intentional relationships. It is unlikely you and your partner initially shared intentional or extended families.

3. Do you have an extended and/or intentional family? If so, who are included in your extended and/or intentional family? Is it identical with your partner's extended and/or intentional family? What are the reasons for any difference? How do you feel about any differences?

4. What are your feelings about your relationships with your extended and/or intentional families?

The fifth question allows you to look at how you are doing at integrating your relationship unit into other groups.

5. Are you included in your partner's family of origin and extended family or intentional family? How do you feel about your current level of inclusion and how that happened?

The sixth and seventh questions give you a look at accomplishments and challenges with all your families and your feelings. Take a moment to celebrate this comprehensive look.

6. List your and your partner's accomplishments relating to your and your partner's family of origin. If you have extended and/ or intentional families, list your accomplishments with them. How do you feel about each of these sets of accomplishments? Does having so many "families" cause feelings? Discuss them with your partner.

7. For each of the families, what difficulties do you have? How do you feel about each of those difficulties?

8. Write down overall feelings, accomplishments, and celebrations for sharing your time as a couple with families, over the last year.

DISCUSS TOGETHER
Together, repeat PEP 7: "Releasing Blocks to Joy," Part 2. This is intended to help you in your continuing process to release blocks to your joy.

Review the "Discussion Guidelines" in Part 3, before sharing. Summarize areas where you both resonate. Make note of any items either of you feel is important.

MAKE YOUR GOALS
Record specific goals that you and your partner agree to commit to, as well as specific actions you and your partner will take, in the

coming year to support your relationships with all your families. As a guide, consider the following:

- **What specific goals for next year, do you both have as a couple relating to all your families and/or individuals in them?** Separate goals by family, each family of origin, and extended and/or intentional families.

- **What specific goals do you each, individually, have relating to your families and/or individuals in them?**

- **What specific actions will you take to support the goals?**

- **What specific actions will you take to support your partner in achieving goals?**

We are often far away from our family of origin and have formed close friends, an "intentional family."

CHAPTER 11:
Our Friends

INTRODUCTION

Our friends are important. Moving into a new relationship can raise questions about where our friends from the past now fit. Focusing on a new relationship can conflict with the time we formerly easily devoted to friends. Each of you likely have different friends. Now you each have relationships with your partner's friends as well, potentially a group of new friends, and their partners. When it comes to our friendships, we each need to make choices about where to focus our time.

People have friends and acquaintances. There is overlap of the two. For the purposes of this chapter, we suggest you limit your thinking to the ten or so closest to you, regardless of whether you consider them friends or acquaintances. Those people you spend time with in sports or community activities may better fit into later chapters, such as Activities. Don't be concerned about agreeing upon who makes the list of friends and acquaintances.

OUR EXPERIENCE

Barb

Mort and I are were surprised to discover we are often drawn to different people! We've had to decide which relationships we want to nurture separately and which together. This hasn't always been easy, especially if one of us had a friend of the opposite sex. We learned about feelings of possessiveness and jealousy. We learned how damaging it was to feel threatened, and we learned to build trust.

At one time, we were attending a Unitarian church where I participated in a women's sexuality discussion group. I found it interesting and supportive. Mort seemed not to understand my need for feminine support and girlfriends.

Mort

 The truth was I was awful at making and keeping friendships with men. Our couple friends were really Barb's women friends who happened to have husbands. Then, I started joining men's discussion groups and that helped me find my own friends.

One year, in our annual review, we realized we had only one couple for friends; all the rest had moved or divorced. We set a goal to find more couple friends. This was harder than we thought, as we wanted all four to like all four. Now we have a number of couple friendships.

PREP WITH A PEP

Refer to PEP 6: "Keeping Our Own Energy Protected," Part 2. This experiment addresses those people who seem to be pulling energy from you. Doing this PEP will help you slow or stop the "chatter" in your head. You will be able to think more clearly both now and at other times.

YOUR UNIQUE VIEW

These questions are focused on you, your friends and acquaintances. Further, the questions explore overlap of each partner's friends and acquaintances and your feelings about them.

Individually, make notes for your answers to the following questions:

The first and second questions allow you to have an overall view of your friends and acquaintances and how they affect you.

1. How do you feel about your friends or acquaintances? List each of them, remembering to limit your thinking to the ten or so closest to you

2. How do you feel about each of your partner's friends or acquaintances?

The third and fourth questions allow you to see where, and when, your friends come from.

3. How many friends or acquaintances have you maintained from before you were partners? What are your feelings about them?

4. How many friends or acquaintances have you made since your relationship formed? Who are they, how did you meet them, and how do you feel about them?

The fifth question allows you to look at the relationship you have with your friends.

5. What are your accomplishments relating to your friends and acquaintances?
Examples could be working, playing, or traveling with friends.

The sixth question opens the opportunity and challenge of having couple friends who are all fun to be with.

6. Which of your friends are part of a couple with whom you and your partner spend time? What are your feelings about each person in the couple?

7. Write down overall feelings, accomplishments, and celebrations for your having and enjoying your friends, as a couple, over the last year.

DISCUSS TOGETHER
Together, repeat PEP 6: "Keeping Our Own Energy Protected," Part 2.

Review the "Discussion Guidelines" in Part 3, before sharing. Summarize areas where you both resonate. Make note of any items either of you feel is important.

MAKE YOUR GOALS
Record specific goals that you and your partner agree to commit to, as well as specific actions you and your partner will take, in the coming year to support your relationships with your friends. As a guide, consider the following:

- **What specific goals for next year, do you have for your relationship with your friends? Be specific and list the friends.**

- What specific goals for next year, do you have for your relationship with your partner's friends?

- What goals do you both have related to friends in common?

- What specific actions will you take to support the goals?

CHAPTER 12:
Pets

INTRODUCTION

Pets are dependent on their humans. While a source of joy and recreation, they also create tasks that need to be fit into a busy day. There are litter boxes and cages to clean, food and water containers to fill, medications to dispense, messes to clean up, and walks at inconvenient hours. In short, they are intelligent creatures who have needs for our time. Carefully consider whether or not owning a pet is a good idea. We fell into the trap of thinking our daughter would learn responsibility by having a pet. We learned there always needs to be a plan to care for our dependent pets when the primary plan doesn't really work.

Pets are very important. Integrating them into your relationship is important. In addition, pets seem to "know" when we are upset, ill, or going away. They may also see themselves in competition with children for your attention, or linked to one child, or one of you, more than another.

Before you begin, jointly agree whether you want pets and which pets you will consider. These questions are focused on you and your partner as people responsible for dependent pets. This becomes more complex with pets where children are involved.

OUR EXPERIENCE

Barb

I grew up with dogs and cats in the house and found lots of joy and companionship in them. Our first pets, as a couple, were a pair of gerbils. Cinnamon and Nutmeg lived in an aquarium in our tiny third floor walkup apartment. I cleaned their cage and fed them. It never occurred to me that Mort might do anything other than enjoy them! Later, as we graduated from college, moved, and had our own home, we had an interesting experience.

We often slept in on weekends, but on this particular Saturday the doorbell rang at 8 A.M. I stumbled to the door and found three small sets of serious young eyes looking up at me. As a group, the children asked, "Will you take care of the cat?" It turned out they had been feeding a stray cat under the backyard deck. She was very shy with people. We had our first cat! We continued feeding and talking to her and named her Fuzz. After months of just sitting outdoors with her when she ate, she began to come closer and eventually allowed herself to come in the house.

My grandfather was a veterinarian, and I grew up knowing how to care for city pets. Mort grew up on a farm and thought animals should live outside. It took some long discussions to decide to include them in our relationship. It also took negotiation about who was doing care, feeding, and training.

Mort

I grew up in the country, where the general rule of thumb was, "People in the house; animals outside."

My childhood dog slept under the back porch and the barn cats slept in the barn. Since Barb and I were both used to having pets but now lived in the city, I had to adjust. Barb pointed out in an annual review that I seemed not to want dependent pets. I agreed. We are cat people and regularly welcome another kitten to our family. We have friends who have dogs and we are happy to welcome their dogs, too, for a week or so.

PREP WITH A PEP

Think about one of your pets. Then think about something you want to happen or will happen, like a friend is coming to visit with their pet. Allow this to form as a picture in your mind. Think about your pet again. In doing this, you will begin to find your pet is in harmony with what happens and will not be surprised, as demonstrated by hiding, barking, messing.

YOUR UNIQUE VIEW

Individually, make notes for your answers to the following questions:

The first question will give you both a look at each other's pet history.

1. Did you have pets when you were growing up? Who cared for them?

The second and third questions bring you up to date and allow you to see how your history repeats (or doesn't).

2. Do you have pets now? If so, did they come with you to the relationship, or join you since your relationship began?

3. Who cares for which pets? How do you feel about that arrangement?

The fourth and fifth questions allow you to step back and see how having pets really works for you. Now that you are in a relationship, this allows you to jointly decide if pets enhance your life or if they require more of your energy than you want to devote to them.

4. How do you feel about each of the pets you have now?

5. Which pets are easy to have in the house and which are less so. How?

The sixth question allows you to plan together how to invite pets into your relationship.

6. If you don't have pets now, do you want one? What kind, and why?

7. Write down overall feelings, accomplishments, and celebrations for your sharing your life with or without pets, over the last year.

DISCUSS TOGETHER

Review the Discussion Guidelines in Part 3, before sharing. Discuss together your experience with the PEP and which pets you used. This will continue to help bring you together in your relationship. Summarize areas where you both resonate. Make note of any items either of you feel is important.

MAKE YOUR GOALS

Record specific goals that you and your partner agree to commit to, as well as specific actions you and your partner will take, in the coming year to support your relationships with your pets. As a guide, consider the following:

- **What specific goals, for next year, do you both have relating to your pets?** Separate goals by each pet and partner.

- **What specific actions will you take to support the goals?**

PART 6
**Focusing Upon
Our World**

CHAPTER 13:
Activities

INTRODUCTION

We like to think of activities as falling into two categories: participatory and spectator. You might be involved in sports, community, artistic, or religious organizations/activities. These interests need to fit into time not already allocated to earning a living, home care, friends, pet care, relationship care, and personal care, including sleep. Working all these items together into a harmonious life really requires cooperation and a strong relationship, as well as some luck, in our experience.

We have learned it is possible to participate practically full time in community, sports, and social activities. Forming a relationship creates yet another activity. This chapter is meant to help you learn about your choices related to where you spend time and energy. While we may once have drawn value from an activity, that may change over time.

OUR EXPERIENCE

Barb
Both of us worked full time and we had a daughter to raise. Fortunately, I was able to stay home for

Kelley's first five years. When I returned to work full time, I felt I had no time for myself. I began to feel resentful, as I had two – or maybe three – full time jobs as housework and child rearing filled every day! Mort and I overloaded ourselves, which left no time for us as a couple. In time, as we began discussing these feelings, we learned to build in time for just us. We began eating out, taking Kelley to animated movies (we still enjoy these now, just the two of us!). Occasionally we went dancing. Now we've learned square dancing. This time gives us a relaxing experience and helps us prioritize our relationship.

Mort
We found that work really filled our days. My company expected we would be active in community organizations or activities. Pretty soon, we didn't see each other much. We began to look at what we received in return and how we felt from the individual activities, in addition to what we could offer. We looked for organizations we both were interested in. We even served together on two non-profit boards. Several times one or both took on board leadership roles in organizations with significant difficulties; we supported each other through these times.

PREP WITH A PEP
Refer to PEP 6: "Keeping Our Own Energy Protected," Part 2. This will help as you participate in activities with many people.

YOUR UNIQUE VIEW
Individually, make notes for your answers to the following questions.

The first, second, and third questions are an inventory of what you now do and the value of these activities to you. As we serve others, we benefit ourselves in important ways. We need to be vigilant to ensure that energy exchange is balanced and harmonious.

1. What personal activities, like sports, hobbies, or exercise, do you participate in, individually? What expectations, for yourself, do you have?

2. What community activities, volunteering, coaching, do you participate in? What expectations, for yourself, do you have?

3. Star the activities you plan to continue. Are there new ways you want to spend your time?

The fourth question looks at your partner's activity time.

4. How do you feel about the personal and community activities your partner participates in, apart from you?

The fifth and sixth questions help you look at what you do together.

5. What personal and/or community activities, volunteering, coaching, do you participate in, together? What expectations do you have? How do you feel about the personal activities and the community activities you do together? Star the activities you both plan to continue. Are there new ways you want to spend your time?

6. What social activities do you and your partner participate in, together? How do you feel about these events and the time involved? What expectations, including fun, did you have? Star the ones you plan to continue. Are there new ways you want to spend your time?

The seventh question looks at social activities which you or your partner separately attend and what feelings occur.

7. What social activities do you or your partner participate in, separately? How do you feel about them? Star the ones you plan to continue. Are there new ways you want to spend your time?

Finally, the eighth question helps you think about how connected you are with your partner.

8. Do you keep a calendar? Is it paper, smart phone or other? Do you share the activity information with your partner?

9. Write down overall feelings, accomplishments, and celebrations for sharing life activities with your partner over the last year.

DISCUSS TOGETHER

Together, repeat PEP 6: "Keeping Our Own Energy Protected," Part 2. This will help you better focus on your feelings and wants for your relationship, separate from what you hear from others. This will continue to bring you together in your relationship.

Review the "Discussion Guidelines" in Part 3, before sharing. Summarize areas where you both resonate. Make note of any items either of you feel is important.

MAKE YOUR GOALS

Record specific goals that you and your partner agree to commit to, as well specific actions you and your partner will take, in the coming year to support your involvement in activities. As a guide, consider the following:

- **Changes you want to make regarding the balance of time among your relationship, family, activities, work, and spiritual life?**

- **Specific expectations you have for your participation in various activities?** What goals do you have related to each activity?

- **Specific areas to investigate, which may better meet your needs at this stage in life?**

- **Specific activities that you and your partner may want to investigate to better meet your joint needs at this stage in life?**

CHAPTER 14:
Business & Work

INTRODUCTION

Whether people have many or few financial resources, they often choose to work. Whether you work for yourself or someone else, you need to be places, interacting with others, and addressing items which lead to stress. Having a partner in your life who is there most everyday with needs and demands can also be stressful. Two-career families, particularly with children, are even more complex and potentially stressful. Success at work, while welcomed, can lead to positions of increasing responsibility. Addressing all these stresses together by doing the Annual Review and Renewal process can help clarify almost everything.

We have learned that we both could easily find our work taking priority in our lives, competing with our relationship. We often found ourselves so busy that we didn't notice support from our partner or missed the opportunity to support our partner in their work.

OUR EXPERIENCE

Barb

It felt to me that Mort prioritized his career over anything else. When our daughter was born, he thought it was my job to care for her. I had to be very adamant about children being "ours," not mine. It took much discussion to decide on our priorities. After a two-and-a-half-year stint in Belgium with Kelley ages three to five, a new puppy and a recent miscarriage, I determined I needed to work. To do what I felt called to, I needed to go to graduate school. We returned to Cincinnati as soon as Mort's job was able to transfer him. I was accepted to two programs, both outside of Cincinnati. I accepted the University of Louisville program. Attending graduate school was a huge stress, as we had to figure out childcare, housework, and homework. That was the first time I had really stood up for myself and chose what I needed to do for myself. We both entered therapy, made changes again, and moved into a more positive balance. We began dividing household responsibilities, and Mort spent more individual time with Kelley. We found more balance with our family life. It took attentiveness right up to our retirements, and still does.

Mort

 Barb followed me around the world with my work and didn't like it. I thought I had no choice. My job affected both of us in many ways. We didn't really celebrate either of our promotions. I missed out on raising our daughter until she was about three. The idea of us supporting each other emerged, as the work became more stressful. Barb once asked me if there was a possibility I could get an assignment I actually had experience to do. Then Barb had a job where the stress was so high that our friends were concerned. The Annual Review and Renewal process pulled us together, got us to say out loud what stressed us, what we wanted, and focused us on solutions. Support in work and business was one of those things I wish we had thought of much earlier in our relationship.

PREP WITH A PEP

Refer to PEP 7: "Releasing Blocks to Joy," Part 2. We often have many rules about how to be at work. If we don't, someone at work will be glad to share rules they are sure we need to know.

YOUR UNIQUE VIEW

Individually, make notes for your answers to the following questions.

The first question is an inventory of what accomplishments you experienced, however you define them.

1. What have each of you accomplished in your work over the last year? Work includes your own in-home or out-of-home business, working out of the home in someone else's business, part-time work, and work creating a home.

The second question asks how you feel about your success.

2. How do you feel about your work accomplishments?

The third question asks you to look at how you celebrate success, i.e. does the success need to be really big, or, or, or?

3. Which work accomplishment(s) did you celebrate? How? When?

In the fourth question, did your partner support you, did you notice, and how did you feel about their support?

4. In what way(s) did your partner support you to help make your achieving these work accomplishments easier? How did you feel about that support?

The fifth question shifts to your views of your partner's successes. Later when you talk together you will learn how observant you and your partner are about each other's successes.

5. What has your partner accomplished in their work over the last year?

In the sixth question, you will have an opportunity to learn how you react to other's successes.

6. How do you feel about your partner's work accomplishments?

In the seventh question, how do you fit into your partner's success celebrations?

7. What work accomplishment(s) were celebrated? How? When?

Finally, in the eighth question, how are you supporting your partner, and are these actions effective?

8. In what way(s) did you support your partner to make achieving these work accomplishments easier? How did they feel about that support?

9. Write down overall feelings, accomplishments, and celebrations for your sharing your life with one or both of you working, over the last year.

DISCUSS TOGETHER

Together, repeat PEP 7: "Releasing Blocks to Joy," Part 2. This PEP allows "rules" you have picked up along the way to move away and be gone. This will allow you to focus on what both of you want and how to get it.

Review the "Discussion Guidelines" in Part 3, before sharing. Summarize areas where you both resonate. Make note of any items either of you feel is important.

MAKE YOUR GOALS

Record specific goals that you and your partner agree to commit to, as well as specific actions you and your partner will take, in the coming year to support your business and work. As a guide, consider the following:

- **What goals do you have for your work over the next year? How can your partner support you? How can you support your partner?**

- **What feelings do you have, now that each of you has these goals and commitments of support?**

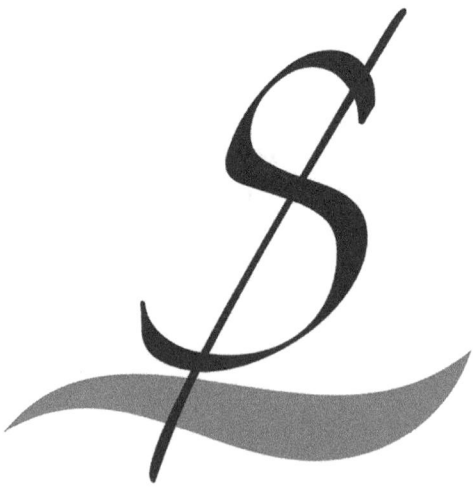

CHAPTER 15:
Finances

INTRODUCTION

We think of money as "frozen energy." It is past energy represented today as paper or lines of type on a computer screen. The money flows in and out of our lives, just as energy does. We believe both partners in relationship need to know where the money (energy) goes to and comes from. Finances are one subject where couples often have trouble communicating and working well together. Also, bills really are notes from people who trust us. They trust we will pay them. For us, we need to know we will, or may be able to, pay our bills, and how.

This topic is one of the more time consuming and often difficult discussion topics, which is why we've structured it with additional questions to help you. You can use some of the previous discussions to support you in this discussion. For example, you might note examples in Chapter 8 in the Personal Responsibilities Summary, such as which of you actually pays the bills.

OUR EXPERIENCE

Barb
Since I am a "big picture, bottom line" thinker, and Mort is a "details, list-creator" thinker, I hated spending

hours reviewing budget decisions when I thought we could do it in a few minutes. It took much practice and deep discussion to figure out how to use both our skills. My parents both worked and had separate money and responsibilities. I wanted some of my own money. In the beginning, we each had separate checking accounts and each contributed to a joint household account. This worked for quite a while and yet, I still felt burdened by it. Finally, we have one checking account. We both have worked to simplify record-keeping, and we review finances together once a quarter unless something unusual occurs. We were able to work it out with some helpful budget tools and Mort's great ability to pay bills on line!

Mort

 I always thought Barb didn't really want to know about money. It turned out I didn't want her to know. She asked really good questions. In later years, we set goals and achieved them. We did, and do, what we want and allow the money to flow to support us. This is a lot different from always being what I call "Lack landers." We used to live in the Land of Lack, saying, "We can't afford it."

When we started using money tracking software, we were better able to assess where the money was going, with great relief on both our parts. See the sample budget or spending plan sheet at the end of the book as a sample plan. We use money tracking software to gather actual spending information to compare with our actual plan. We did this task manually for years. Actually, I did.

PREP WITH A PEP

Refer to PEP 3: "Centering," Part 2. Also, refer to PEP 5: "Connecting to Unlimited Energy." Together, these PEPs will help you stay in the present and have access to additional energy as needed. Refer to PEP 7: "Releasing Blocks to Joy" as a way of considering which rules to follow and where to create new ones for you.

YOUR UNIQUE VIEW

Individually, make notes for your answers to the following questions.

The first, second, and third questions relate to your net worth. Think of your net worth as how much energy (or money) you have accumulated. Of course, this changes over time.

1. What is your net worth? How do you feel about knowing this? Net worth is what you have (house, car, investments, etc.) minus what you owe. Review the example at the end of this chapter.

2. Is your net worth changing? Upwards? Downwards? Do you know the reason for the change? You will likely better know this as you continue your Annual Review & Renewal Approach over several years.

3. How do you feel about this change?

The fourth and fifth questions ask you to consider money (energy) you have saved to live on when you are not working. Type "retirement calculator" into an internet search engine and use one of the free calculators to determine the amount needed based on your assumptions. A retirement planner can do this as well, usually for a fee. We recommend the book "Intersection of Joy and Money" written by Mackey McNeil, which provides some innovative ways to plan about money.[14]

4. What amount, if any, do you already have to support you in retirement?

[14] Mackey Miriam McNeil, The Intersection of Joy and Money (Ft. Wright, KY: Prosperity Publishing, 2002).

5. Is it changing? How do you feel about this change?
The sixth and seventh questions look at income and expense as it is not reasonable or desirable to live for long beyond your income.

6. Is your income more or less than your spending? To determine this, complete the sample budget or spending plan at the end of the book.

7. How do you feel about this situation?

The eighth through twelfth questions ask you to look at how you manage money in your relationship on a daily basis.

8. What is your philosophy about handling money: mine, yours, ours.

9. How do you handle combined expenses? Do you have one bank account to pay all expenses? Do you have one bank account combining parts of two incomes to fund "common" expenses like mortgage and utilities? Or do you have separate bank accounts?

10. What other ways have you examined?

11. How do you feel about the way you have chosen?

12. Who is responsible for your different financial activities, such as paying bills, buying food, buying miscellaneous items, or clothing? How do you feel about that division of responsibilities?

The thirteenth and fourteenth questions ask you to look at how you manage money.

13. What significant spending have you had in the last year? How did you decide to fund those items?

14. How do you feel about your decision making regarding income and spending?

15. Write down overall feelings, accomplishments, and celebrations for your financial health, over the last year.

DISCUSS TOGETHER

Together, repeat PEP 3: "Centering," Part 2. Together, repeat PEP 5: "Connecting to Unlimited Energy." Together, repeat PEP 7: "Releasing Blocks to Joy." These allow you both to become centered, clear and filled continuously with energy.

Review the "Discussion Guidelines" in Part 3, before sharing. Summarize areas where you both resonate. Make note of any items either of you feel is important.

MAKE YOUR GOALS

Record specific goals that you and your partner agree to commit to, as well as specific actions you and your partner will take, in the coming year related to:

- **Income**
- **Retirement**
- **Expense (any major expenses planned?)**
- **Are income and expenses balanced?**
- **Are changes needed to have "enough?"**

SUMMARIZE YOUR FINANCIAL SITUATION

The following net worth example is intended to help you think about your financial situation. As we said, we use money tracking software as a tool and it calculates all this sort of information. It also allows us to fill in our spending plan/budget. Please see the end of the book for a sample budget or spending plan.

Your net worth may be significantly different than the example, but no matter the amount, we believe you need to know what it is. We certainly needed to. In the beginning, your net worth may be less than zero. Ours was $428 and a small diamond ring. This form is intended to provide ideas about what you can change.

EXAMPLE

Net Worth (Date)

Asset	Value
Cash and Bank Accounts	
Partner 1 Checking	$1000
Partner 2 Checking	$1500
Common Checking	$2000
Cash	$250
Savings	$7000
Total Cash and Bank Accounts	**$11750**
Other Assets	
House (Sale Price, rather than purchase price)	$150,000
Furniture, clothing, etc. (Sale Price)	$5000
Car 1	$15000
Car 2	$10000
Boat	$2000
Partner 1 Life Insurance cash value	$11000
Jewelry (Sale Price)	$5000
Total Other Assets	**$198,000**
Investments	
Partner 1 IRA	$40000
Partner 2 IRA	$25000
Stock from Partner 1's Grandpa	$10000
Other stock	$5000
Partner 2's Grandma's coin collection	$10000

Total Investments	**$90000**
Total Assets	**$299,750**
Liabilities	
Credit Cards	
Visa	$6000
American Express	$1000
MasterCard	$3000
Total Credit Cards	**$10000**
Other Liabilities	
Car 1 loan	$10000
House	$120000
School Loan	$50000
Total Other Liabilities	**$180,000**
Total Liabilities	**$190,000**
Net Worth	**$109,750**

See end of book for blank Net Worth forms which you can copy. Also at the end is a blank budget planning form, intended to help you summarize where you spend your money.

The money flows in and out of our lives, just as energy does.

CHAPTER 16:
Vacations and Travel

INTRODUCTION

Work provides people with structured routines that can be both comforting and stressful. We must wake at a certain time, arrive to work or activities at a certain time, pick up the children, feed or walk the pets, and prepare our meals. Vacations, while potentially fun, also teach us how much we depend on that structure for life to run smoothly. Vacationing with your partner in the early days of your relationship, combined with a sudden lack of structure, can make for a less than pleasant experience. Planning and sharing expectations and wants will really help make this a fun time.

During vacations and travel, the daily structure changes dramatically. This may allow some couples to really enjoy each other in a way they can't during the normal routines of daily life. For other couples, in addition to the fun of traveling, it is also possible to become stressed on vacation, with different rules, expectations, and so on. Vacation and travel may be a test of our relationship's flexibility, showing us places to improve while being in new environments.

One young man differentiates between a "vacation" and a "visit." He says, "Sometimes a visit to friends or family doesn't really feel like a vacation, so I always make sure to be clear with myself whether I'm taking a vacation or making a visit. That helps me be clear with my expectations."

You may discover some crossover between the questions related to family, holidays, and travel.

OUR EXPERIENCE

Barb

This is a fun topic! Through our vacations and travel, Mort and I dreamed and created visions. We have traveled a lot, and have enjoyed it both because we knew what each other wanted from the trip and because we had both helped to create it! Mort is a super planner, while I'm more spontaneous and happy to just pack and go. Our first big trip was to Europe after we graduated from college and before we had jobs, a house, and children. We had three weeks to see all of it on five dollars a day! Mort did the research, and I concurred. Still, I missed the spontaneity of just exploring. We had a wonderful time and exercised our flexibility when a workers' strike forced us to reroute to Portugal. I was happy about this unplanned adventure! We still follow this pattern of Mort planning and me concurring. I state my wants and find ways to build in spontaneity. Recently, we went to Ireland for a week. We stayed in bed and breakfasts not booked until that day, ate in places we discovered along the way, and drove around on the 'wrong' side of the road and sometimes got lost. Mort was comfortable with less structure, and I too was more relaxed.

Mort

 We both have had jobs that involved traveling, sometimes a lot! As a result, much of our traveling for vacation was included in business travel. Travel not connected to work required thought for me to develop enthusiasm for spending even more time on an airplane. Normally, vacations involved either going home to Nebraska to visit family or to the beach to collapse.

I always had more vacation time than Barb. Barb temporarily stopped working to have children, so I spent my excess vacation time traveling with our daughter in the summer. We traveled for two to three weeks each year, when she was ages 8 to 17. This solidified my relationship with our daughter and we had fun!

We see vacation and travel as a joint experience, more so since we retired. I like traveling with Barb as she notices things that I don't. Her observations – like the sweet smell of flower markets or the angelic sound of singing rehearsal in a cathedral – are my gain.

PREP WITH A PEP

Refer to PEP 3: "Centering," Part 2. Allow this PEP to draw your focus toward your relationship on vacation being different than daily life.

YOUR UNIQUE VIEW

Individually, make notes for your answers to the following questions regarding how you vacationed and traveled last year.

The first question is an inventory of what you did over the last year. One or both of you may travel for work or family needs.

1. Where did you vacation? For how long? Did you travel with other people? Include long weekends, day trips, and more, as well as other travel, such as visiting family, business, or conferences. How much did you travel together?

The second question asks you to look together at your feelings about each of your vacation and travel times. Did you have fun or did you feel disappointed about something. What?

2. How do each of you feel about the time you spent together on vacation, as well as other travel?

The third and fourth questions are an opportunity to look at your goals and accomplishments for your vacation and travel time. Remember, the goal for much vacation and travel is to rest and renew.

3. What specific goals did you and your partner have for each vacation and travel time?

4. What were your accomplishments and appreciations related to your goals for vacation and travel?

5. Write down overall feelings, accomplishments, and celebrations for your vacations and traveling over the last year.

DISCUSS TOGETHER

Together, repeat PEP 3: "Centering," Part 2. This will help you better focus on your feelings and wants for your relationship, separate from the pulls and obligations that you "hear" from others.

Review the "Discussion Guidelines" in Part 3, before sharing. Summarize areas where you both resonate. Make note of any items either of you feel is important.

MAKE YOUR GOALS

Record specific goals that you and your partner agree to commit to, as well as specific actions you and your partner will take, in the coming year to support vacation and travel. As a guide, consider the following:

- **What do you plan to do in the coming year regarding vacation and travel?**

- **What goals do you have for each item of travel? Who will participate?**

- **Are there new places or ways to spend your time together away from your daily life? What goals do you have for these? Who will take the lead in arranging these?**

CHAPTER 17:
Holidays and Special Occasions

INTRODUCTION

Holidays bring an opportunity for lots of fun – and stress. Your family may expect that you will join a holiday celebration just as you did before you were in a committed relationship. Looking at this situation ahead of time can prevent misunderstandings and provides a place for you to behave as a couple in setting your own boundaries. If your family members live in opposite directions, you will need to choose where you spend your holiday. If and when you have children, and still have parents, this will become something to really plan well.

We have learned we **can** organize our current lives around holiday and other celebrations with family or friends from the past. The pull of what we have always done is almost irresistible. We find it easy to just sort of keep doing what we did when we were single. It is important to decide what and how we celebrate. This helps create our own way of being in our relationship. The value of certain celebrations may change over time, and it is helpful to honor that change.

OUR EXPERIENCE

Barb

Holidays can be frantic or hectic. Early in our mar- riage, we ran from family to family, spent lots of time on the road to Nebraska, and returned exhausted to our home in Ohio. We would load up Kelley, all her gifts and ours, and pile into the car to drive through snow and ice to be "home" for the holidays. We started discussing how **we** wanted holidays to be and began to structure our plans to meet those desires. We stopped traveling for holidays and established new traditions with our selected intentional family. We began to experience meaningful, peaceful times at our home! Our families were not happy, but we now had created our own home, with our own traditions. We traded winter travel for summer trips to Nebraska.

Mort

In the early days, we spent our time running from family to family for Christmas. We had an especially hard time giving up Nebraska for Christmas. Weather wise, it was a terrible time to drive. We began to celebrate some holidays with our intentional family and created our own traditions. Later, we flew to our daughter's home in San Francisco for Christmas. She was 34 the first time we did this, and she was thrilled. Birthdays, holidays, graduations, or basketball games followed by a shared meal are all easy ways to create opportunities to connect with nearby friends and family.

PREP WITH A PEP

Refer to PEP 7: "Releasing Blocks to Joy," Part 2. Also, refer to PEP 6: "Keeping Our Own Energy Protected."

When completing the Releasing Blocks to Joy PEP, focus on any celebration in the last year that you now feel unsettled about. Think "This celebration was important and I believe I 'should' have gone." Then start the Releasing Blocks to Joy PEP.

YOUR UNIQUE VIEW

Individually, make notes for your answers to the following questions.

The first and second questions are an inventory of what you now do and the value to you.

1. What holidays and celebrations did you attend this last year:
    a. What holidays did you celebrate throughout the last year?
    b. Together or separately? What other celebrations did you participate in?
    c. Who did you celebrate them with? In what way?
    d. Did you have specific goals about celebrations?

2. How do you feel about those celebrations now?
    a. How do you feel about **each** of these celebrations? Were they in general uplifting, or not, for both of you?
    b. How do you feel about being, or not being, included in your partner's holiday celebrations?
    c. Did you meet your goals relating to celebrating holidays and celebrations?

The third question asks you to envision together how you will spend your time and energy in holiday and other celebrations. You may still celebrate separately. Choosing this approach may make the most sense to both of you.

3. What celebrations and holidays do you plan to partici-pate in for the coming year? What specific goals do you have? As a couple? Individually?

The fourth question asks about alternate ways to celebrate with others, opening more opportunities for other ways to spend your time. The idea of having goals for holiday and other celebrations may seem new. We use it as a way to separate those we attend, and those we choose not to attend. We may choose to be involved in ways different than attending. As we grow older, our goal sometimes is as simple as "this may be our last time to visit with a relative or friend."

4. Celebrating other than with your presence
    a. Do you celebrate, at a distance, by sending cards and letters, or using webcam, recordings, or other ideas?
    b. What holidays or events will you recognize with cards or letters?
    c. Who of the two of you leads this work?

5. Write down overall feelings, accomplishments, and celebrations for sharing holidays and special occasions with your partner over the last year.

DISCUSS TOGETHER
Together, repeat PEP 7: "Releasing Blocks to Joy," Part 2. Together, repeat PEP 6: "Keeping Our Own Energy Protected." These will help you better focus on your feelings and wants for your relationship, separate from the pulls and obligations that you "hear" from others.

Review the "Discussion Guidelines" in Part 3, before sharing. Summarize areas where you both resonate. Make note of any items either of you feel is important.

MAKE YOUR GOALS
Record specific goals that you and your partner agree to commit to, as well as specific actions you and your partner will take, in the

coming year to support your holidays and special occasion. As a guide, consider the following:

- Holiday and other celebrations you want to be involved in, both together and separately. What are your goals for each?

- Are there opportunities to combine attending some celebrations with other wants, such as vacation?

- What holidays and other celebrations do you no longer plan to attend? Who will communicate these changes?

- Which holidays and other celebrations do you want to participate in that focus on your relationship? Some of these may be new. What are your goals for these celebrations?

- What do you want to participate in in ways other than with your presence? What are your goals for this?

CHAPTER 18:
End of Life Planning

INTRODUCTION

After we wrote the first complete draft of this Workbook, we asked several different types of couples to review it. From this review, we realized we needed to include a section on End of Life, aka Death. In our personal experience, this is a big, important discussion in a relationship.

Depending on your stage of life, some loved ones will have already died. Death discussions in a relationship may range from a simple sharing of each other's end of life experiences, such as the logistical and emotional effects related to the deaths of loved ones. We may bear witness to the deaths of our parents, grandparents, friends, even our and other's children. This section is set up to support this conversation. Doing this work will ease the effect of the death of friends, other's children and their parents.

We don't know what actually happens in death. We do know that the physical presence of the person is gone and we must reorder our lives. If there is time, the person leaving may need support and caring past the medical profession's capability.

Additionally, this chapter asks you and your partner to think about, prepare for, and make agreements related to your own deaths. An interfaith couple we have worked with found it important to discuss the differences in their interment wishes, as did a couple who practiced a different faith than their families of origin. Other couples have spent time discussing what to do if one partner needs support and caring past the medical profession's capability. This section guides you and your partner through a discussion about your wishes related to your own dying and post-death wishes.

As we consider end of life, there seem to be three possibilities for preparation:

1. Make no preparation for your wishes.
2. Prepare by informally stating (verbally) what you desire.
3. Prepare your wishes in writing and share with your partner and, perhaps, with others.

This section is about clarifying, planning and easing what will happen. As Mort often says, we should focus on dying at the slowest possible rate. However, we must accept that the end of life will come.

OUR EXPERIENCE

Barb

Death, in general, feels like a natural occurrence to me when it comes after a long life or illness. Having time to say what I need to, time to say goodbye, feels comforting to me. When death occurred suddenly to my loved ones, like it did with the death of our dear daughter Kelley in a freak drowning accident, I felt deep shock. I was devastated and unprepared. I walked in an emotional fog of grief and regret. It was immeasurably helpful to have Kelley's written wishes to rely on, as we were lost. This is why I think preparation is important.

Mort

Losing someone close is a blow in all the ways possible. To make it worse, often we need to make choices, such as burial or cremation, and plan a ritual for ourselves and others to attend. We also need to decide whether to give away some or all of that person's things, and when. When this happened with our daughter, we were lost until her friend turned up a "Thinking about my death" document Kelley had written years before. I had seen it and didn't remember it. We followed it. And, very importantly, two of her friends accompanied us as we walked through interment choices of caskets, urns, and many more. We didn't know. We were numb.

After Kelley's "celebration of life," people told us it was the most uplifting wonderful ceremony they had ever attended. We are grateful to our friends who organized it. We gave away her professional books, jewelry, and clothes right away, mostly to her school, friends, and family. We kept her writings, personal books, and other stuff until we felt we could look in the boxes. For five years, we didn't even know what was in there.

Shortly after our daughter died, one of our cats went missing (or so we thought). Turns out, she was hiding in the dense woods from predators. She reappeared several days later to our great relief and joy. We were surprised at how we went a bit "nuts" at this perceived loss so fresh on the heels of our daughter's death. The sensation of loss lurked just beneath the surface for us for a long time. Loss can be a big deal. Loss reminds us every time of other losses. That's how our memories and minds work.

PREP WITH A PEP

Together, repeat PEP 1: "Balancing and Releasing Other's Energies, Part 2," and sitting some distance apart. Also, refer to PEP 3: "Centering." You may want to revisit these PEPs as you work through this topic. These will help you stay in the present and see what **you** want. Reacquaint yourself with PEP 2: "Paraphrasing" to help you ensure you understand your partner.

YOUR UNIQUE VIEW

Before answering the questions below, consider your understanding of the end of life. If you have no idea, or really don't want to think about the end of your life, consider talking with a friend or spiritual leader regarding their ideas.

Individually, make notes for your answers to the following questions. Leaving people with no clear instructions about what you want for your death can be difficult for them.

1. What kind of end of life care would you like?

a. Hospice, either at your home or in a facility? This offers an opportunity for you and others to gather together, although they may be able to at a hospital as well, depending on time available.

b. Do you want life support, either short term or "forever"?

c. Completing a living will and a medical power of attorney will help you navigate the jargon.

d. When in the hospital, do you want extraordinary medical measures to help preserve your life? Again, the documents mentioned in item c. above and later in this chapter will help with the jargon.

2. How do you want your life to be celebrated? Celebrated at all? If so, how, when, where? There is a large range of possibilities, from nothing, to traditional funerals, to wakes, to out-and-out celebrations of life. Since these celebrations serve the ones remaining, something will probably happen, particularly if you don't leave ideas for others. Our experience is that this time is much easier for others when there are some guidelines from the one now missing.

3. What would you like to have happen with your body? Again, there is a large range of possibilities, from organ, bone, and skin donation, donation to a medical research organization, cremation, or burial. The truth is you are done with your body, regardless of what you believe happens after death. With cremation, the ashes will still exist, possibly for future disposal. Your spiritual leader or a funeral director can help with this when you are able to make the choice.

4. How would you like to have your body honored? Possibilities range from casket choice, to cremation urn, to types of flowers, types of music, and any number of choices. Funeral directors are helpful as long as those remaining have clear-eyed friends helping to choose. You can preselect these things as well with funeral directors and services. Mort's Mom and Dad did this, which allowed us to focus on honoring and grieving.

5. Financial. This is also a big deal. Do you have a power of attorney, a medical power of attorney, a living will, a will? Yes or no? If not, go do this. See an attorney. Dying without these documents puts an extraordinary burden on your survivors. Young people need wills, too. Our daughter didn't have one. Then, we **did** need a lawyer! The forms for most are on the web, and living will forms are also available at hospitals. As a start, consider these sites to lead you through making these documents:

> a. Will
> (**http://www.wikihow.com/Write-Your-Own-Last-Will-and-Testament**). If there are assets and children, we suggest considering consulting an attorney to ensure the paperwork is correct. Ensure you sign it correctly; a friend didn't and it wasn't valid.

> b. Medical Power of Attorney & Living Will
> (**http://www.lawdepot.com/contracts/living-will-medical-power-of-attorney/**) or a local hospital.

> c. Power of Attorney (**http://www.lawdepot.com/contracts/power-of-attorney-forms/**). Again, an attorney can be very helpful.

6. Do you care what happens to your possessions? Your survivors may care, and knowing your wishes can help them. Leaving lists of specific items to go to specific people or organizations is helpful. Have you made such ideas known in writing? Do so now and share your written wishes. Barb's mom did this and the list was lost. Sigh. Mort's mom did as well and the list was found. Whew!

DISCUSS TOGETHER

Together, repeat PEP 1: "Balancing and Releasing Other's Energies, Part 2" and sitting some distance apart. Together, repeat PEP 3: "Centering." Together, repeat PEP 2: "Paraphrasing." These will help you stay in the present and see what **you** want. Be ready to use the paraphrase process as you discuss. This will help you better understand what your partner is wanting to communicate. See how this helps cut to the real meaning and stops the "self-accelerating-go-to-hell system."

Review the "Discussion Guidelines" in Part 3, before sharing. Summarize areas where you both resonate. Make note of any items either of you feel is important.

MAKE YOUR GOALS

Record specific goals that you and your partner agree to commit to, as well as specific actions you and your partner will take, in the coming year to support End of Life planning. As a guide, consider the following:

- **What specific goals will you and your partner commit to? What do you plan to continue, add, or change for the coming year? You may have identified specific choices that need to be researched. List each.**

- **What actions will you and your partner take, in the coming year to support your goals and each other as you achieve them? List them.**

PART 7
Our Future Planning

CHAPTER 19:
Our Vision for the Coming Year

INTRODUCTION

Developing your vision for the coming year asks you to imagine a future you want to work toward together with your partner. This may sound like a big thing to organize. Creating a vision for ourselves is both challenging and fun. It provides a direction for what we do. The energy for our relationship flows from our vision and fills our relationship. We know we are energetic beings using our energy in many ways every day. Our vision helps us by providing an overall direction for us. Our responsibility is both to hold the vision and to conduct our lives and our relationship accordingly. These visions are usually fairly simple. Ordering our lives according to them, is less simple. We think it is far better to move in the direction we envision, than moving through life doing what shows up as we used to do. Being in charge is better for us and way more fun.

OUR EXPERIENCE

Barb & Mort
Creating a vision statement for the year ahead first seemed a bit corporate, as we had to do this for the organizations

where we worked. Over time, we both began to see how visions energized and guided us at work. So, we applied visioning in our lives. It's a bit like dreaming the life and future you want.

Our Mutual Vision for the last several years has been:

Change and simplify our life.

Barb
My Personal vision for the year:

Love every day in many ways. Be creative, joyful, present, positive, forgiving, open and willing. Teach, share, learn and grow.

While my personal vision doesn't use the word simplify, it supports simplifying by creating space for changing and simplifying.

Mort
My Personal vision for the year:

Create a world with circles of joy, wellness and power by unconditionally loving and trusting myself and others.

This vision offers the energy to change my life by reducing stress in my life in the first place. This stress sucks up my energy and makes it harder to change.

What these personal visions do is support our mutual vision to encourage, or even demand, adjusting and simplifying our lives, as we set specific ways to achieve our personal visions.

PREP WITH A PEP

Refer to PEP 3: "Centering," Part 2. This will help you stay in the present and see what **you** want. Also, refer to PEP 5: "Connecting to Unlimited Energy." This work of creating a vision may be new ground and unlimited energy will be helpful.

YOUR UNIQUE VIEW

Before answering the questions below, consider searching the worldwide web for something like "creating a personal vision." There are checklists and guidelines. Be cautious to stay on the personal side rather than business side.

Individually, make notes for your answers to the following questions. Please be aware that your personal vision and what you determine as your mutual vision, while related, may be different. See our examples above. Also, while our personal visions adjust most years, the mutual vision seems to last us for several years.

The first and second questions ask you to focus on yourself and create a sample vision. We have changed our visions over time, so consider this first one to be an experiment.

1. What do you personally want to be, see, and/or have in five years? Ignore practicality for now. You may want to include your immediate family.

2. Summarize the above in one sentence (see our example above). Sometimes, practicality will want to sneak in. Work to keep the vision something you can see as attainable in the future, although not yet convertible to a worklist.

The third and fourth questions ask you to focus on the two of you as you develop a mutual vision.

3. What do you as a couple want to be, see, and/or have in five years? Ignore practicality for now. You may want to include your immediate family.

4. Summarize your answer to question three in one sentence. Sometimes, practicality will want to sneak in. Work to keep the vision something you can see as attainable in the future, although not yet convertible to a worklist.

DISCUSS TOGETHER

Together, repeat PEP 3: "Centering," Part 2. Together, repeat PEP 2: "Paraphrasing." These will help you stay in the present and see what **you** want. Be ready to use the paraphrase process as you discuss. This will help you better understand what your partner is wanting to communicate. Together, repeat PEP 5: "Connecting to Unlimited Energy." This creating a vision may be new ground and unlimited energy will be helpful.

Share your personal visions and discuss how you want to experiment with the one you chose. Note this is for understanding and support rather than approval.

Share your ideas for a mutual vision. You each may have more than one suggestion. Allow a mutual vision to grow from the discussion. You may need to create several practice visions and just be with them for a bit.

When you select personal and mutual visions, be sure you each understand one another's vision as well as your mutual vision. Also, you may want to revisit them throughout the year.

MAKE YOUR GOALS

Record your personal visions, as well as the vision that you and your partner agree to commit to. As a guide, consider the following:

- What is your mutual vision?

- What goals do you have regarding the use of your mutual vision for the coming year?

- What are your individual personal visions?

- What goals do you have regarding the use of your individual personal vision for the coming year?

- How will you keep the visions in mind?

- How often will you revisit them through the year?

CHAPTER 20:
Our Goals for the Coming Year

INTRODUCTION

Using the Annual Review and Renewal process results in the creation of numerous goals related to improving your relationship. This chapter asks you to identify and choose specific goals for the coming year to achieve your visions. These goals become the center of our lives, and our intentions to improve and change in a planned way give us strength and creativity. The goals we finally choose usually relate in some way to our vision, but not always.

In the early days of completing our Annual Review & Renewal process, we learned it is possible to identify more goals than seem reasonable. Remember there is next year and a year after that, and so on. We suggest you **identify the most important goals**, changes, or improvements that will make a real difference in your relationship with each other and your relationship with the world where you live. Remember the world you see in your vision.

OUR EXPERIENCE

Barb & Mort

We have been setting goals since our very first Annual Review & Renewal. As we gained experience with this process, our goals became a collection (and refinement) of the goals we developed for each topic, summarized and listed in one place. We keep them handy to refer to in the kitchen. Some years we don't refer to them, and they still seem to get done. We have seen a greater than 85% completion rate year after year.

We shared our goals with our daughter from about age seven onward. In later years, she said "I don't understand. You set goals for the year, and then they are done by summer!?" Intentions, which are goals, seem to be important.

Barb

When we began the Annual Review & Renewal, I had a tough time with setting goals. I had to work to remember they are steps to get me moving toward what I want.

Mort

Barb and I had set goals all through our relationship. When we

decided we wanted to do something – like air condition our top-floor apartment in an old house in Nebraska – we just set about getting it done. Our goals and action items were not two separate things. The idea of looking at many parts of our lives and addressing goals simultaneously was new and fun, once I got used to it.

PREP WITH A PEP

Use your experience with the PEPs to select the ones that will best help you sort through the goals coming from your Annual

Review & Renewal process. As you sort through them, select the ones most important to improving and strengthening your relationship.

YOUR UNIQUE VIEW

First look at the goals that you both identified in each chapter. Not all chapters may have goals. The work is to identify goals that will most easily build your relationship in a fun way. This may be all of them or just some of them. This thinking ahead is intended to help you get clear on what is most important to you and the reasons. Make a list of what you chose.

DISCUSS TOGETHER

Share the PEPs you chose and select one or more to do as you start the discussion.

Share your goals lists together, marking goals you both support. Then, discuss the differences in goals. Select the goals you both will commit to achieve, or work toward, in the coming year. Any other goals will still be listed in each chapter's notes for consideration after discussion of the topic next year.

Consider also making overarching goals for each topic rather than many detail goals. For example, a goal might be, "We will participate in each child's activities. Refer to the detailed summary." Then list the goal by child.

We have found it important to understand the reason each of us chose the goals we did. Learning more about how the other thinks, feels, and cares fosters intimacy.

Some goals we had to support one year's vision were:
Join and participate in organizations giving us access to people we

can love every day in many ways. Barb sings with Threshold Choir at hospice units and other places. She helps more people become qualified to sing. Both Barb and Mort participate in prayer and healing teams supporting people in many parts of the world. Mort supports senior men through the Mankind Project. Mort focuses in our business with people suffering from traumatic events. Helping people with these experiences often easily allows their lives to work much better. See www.NicholsonPEP.com

Other examples of goals include:

Downsize from our large home to a more manageable home.

Have a cabin built for summer living.

Do the above two goals all in one year rather than over several years.

Detach from material "stuff." We gave a lot away and had a Native American, First Nation style "give away" for our friends to take away "stuff." We see some of it in their homes. Still, we purchased a couple items when we moved into a new home.

Simplify, simplify, simplify. We released many tasks by moving to a smaller and easier to care for condo. We have automated almost all bill paying. We recycle, are energy conservationists, and purchased a hybrid car, which is paying for itself through gas not purchased.

Focus travel on a second home. The cabin was built far enough away that it requires us, and friends, to be organized to get there. Our focus is on simplicity and nature. We are minimizing other vacation and travel.

MAKE YOUR GOALS

- Record your goals. As a guide, consider the following:

- **What goals do you both have for the coming year?** Capture these from the discussion, so you have a clear list of your intentions. These will be useful to refer to regularly.

- **In addition to actions related to specific goals from each chapter, are there any other specific actions will you take to support the goals?** For example, review the goals and the action needed to support them. You may want to do this in your weekly meeting, once per month, or at another separate meeting.

- **Do you have individual goals for the coming year outside of the goal summary from the first question above?** We have not had this happen, but we are only one couple. If so, what are the additional goals? Add them to the overall goal list. What action is needed by each of you to support these added goals?

PART 8
How to Keep
This Going

How to Keep This Going

CONTINUE BUILDING AND STRENGTHENING YOUR RELATIONSHIP

Congratulations! You have finished working together through the chapters, learning ways to manage your personal energy. Now what? Resist the urge to complete the Annual Review & Renewal Process more than once a year. In our experience, more than once a year is unnecessary. It takes time for things to unfold. We have found, however, that **weekly meetings, a monthly check in,** and a **midyear assessment** help us keep on track.

THE WEEKLY "MEETING"

We suggest you schedule a short weekly meeting with a specific agenda to keep the relationship moving in the direction you want it to go. Some people suggest meeting more or less often. We experimented. Once per week works best for us, as we have active lives. This is a set aside "appointment" time to appreciate each other, exchange information, and discuss things that seem "off" to each of us. With our schedules, it is hard to respect the meeting times, even though they last only an hour once a week. We have been doing this for about fifteen years.

We meet at the kitchen table most often, sometimes outside, and sometimes curled up in soft chairs. Pick a location that will support you in staying focused and present with your partner. If you have children, finding a place where you will not be interrupted may require joint creativity. Explaining to older children that you need "couple time" often works, and they can easily entertain themselves. With younger ones, consider meeting during nap time or after their early bedtime. Consider a day or evening out with each other.

The agenda is simple and flexible. We suggest starting with these items for a few months. We found they met our needs and stayed with them. Our experience is that **discussing the items in this order is important**. If you want to add other topics, think together how such additions will enhance your relationship. We resist adding items as they interrupt the flow and make the meeting last over an hour. We don't like that. The weekly meeting helps to catch any short term "drift" away from our agreements.

WEEKLY MEETING AGENDA ITEMS

1. Appreciations. One of us starts with something they appreciate about the other. This may be a quality or something they did. The response is "Thank You." **No other response is encouraged.** Each one shares one appreciation in turn, until we run out. A minimum of five each is ideal though. It has been a week, after all!

2. Sharing information. This always includes sharing our calendars. We added evenings we would cook together, times we could carpool to the same event, attend an event the other is doing, and so on. In fact, sometimes one goes with the other and waits (take a book). These opportunities would be missed without talking through the calendar. Looking ahead more than a month gets a bit tedious for us. There is other information, like news about children, friends, or household maintenance. This keeps us working with the same information.

3. Confusions: This allows us to identify something the other has done, is doing, or is planning to do that confuses us. Frankly, it may also upset us. Using this process takes the sting out of the event for both of us. Now that we have become used to this process and each other, we will bring up confusions as they happen rather than wait. This is a powerful way to work together. Often, we did something, or are planning something, without really thinking through how it will affect the other. We can then make corrections. Confusion is a much less threatening word than "why."

4. Adjustment Requests: These requests often follow the discussion about confusions, but not always. This provides a space in our life for one of us to say they desire a minor adjustment, like "Please don't screw on the mouthwash cap so tightly. My thumb hurts, and I struggle to open it." The other one of us thought it was good to keep it tight so it wouldn't leak if knocked over. This had been going on for about two years. Sometimes, the desired adjustments are larger, such as, "Please don't interrupt me when I am telling a story. I feel discounted." That one led to Mort getting hearing aids to be better able to hear when someone is talking. Sometimes nothing other than being heard will happen. It **is** a request after all.

5. Near-Term Goals: This gives each of us time to share what we plan to do or be, in the next week(s). Short term, it is a way for us to join in some activities, like "this is the week to cut the ornamental grass," or in time off doing nothing. When we each had our plans, unintentionally hidden from the other, we would often get in the other's way. This caused anger, frustration, and loud discussions. Joining together to help one another is so much more fun!

MONTHLY CHECK-INS AND/OR MIDYEAR ASSESSMENTS

Once a month, we look at the goals from the Annual Review & Renewal to review any goals or topics that seem to be an issue. This may result in separate discussions, as needed. Allow your review of your goal progress to both be a summary to stay focused, and a departure point for further discussion.

Alternately (or additionally), you might consider a midyear assessment of your goals. You will have a few goals that are really important. Waiting a year to check in on them may be too long. Also, please decide for yourselves what works best.

BE FLEXIBLE & ALLOW CHANGE

This process has expanded and contracted over the years. For example, we have added whole topics we had not considered, the most recent being the chapter on death. We have chosen in some years to not review goals regularly. We still seemed to achieve them, but we feel more comfortable looking at them monthly to ensure the action plans get integrated into our lives.

In the early days, we spent a lot of time "negotiating" change, assuming we did not have similar goals. The subjects are arranged in the order we discuss them. We have added subjects over the years and changed the order. These differences in our processes from the beginning to more recent times are astounding. You may be astonished too as you use and adjust the Annual Review & Renewal process.

YEAR TWO AND BEYOND!

When completing the Annual Review & Renewal Process in year two and beyond, you will have experience with the process and a set of goals to provide the foundation for some of the discussion subjects for the immediate past year. You also have a vision.

The Annual Review & Renewal process is the same as you have done, with the following additions.

As you answer the questions, first alone, and then ---as a couple, do PEP 3: "Centering," Part 2 and also, PEP 5: "Connecting to Unlimited Energy." These will move you easily into considering how the last year went relative to your goals.

First consider alone your goals and assess how you did on each one. This will actually go quickly. It is likely you will have:

- completed the goal,
- accomplished the goal, in part
- somehow just didn't do it (blew it off), or
- intentionally decided to not do it

Individually, look at how you did regarding your goals. Develop an overall sense of how you did in a sort of a one to ten feeling.

Go to each individual discussion subject. **Consider doing some or all of the listed PEPs, then assess how you did on each goal you set, if any, for each discussion subject.** Use the same sorting mentioned above. Look at how you did. Assess if there are any goals you would like to renew for the coming year, as is, or changed.

Looking at your goals for each discussion subject will easily move you into the questions for that discussion subject. Similar to last year, individually create new answers for each question in each discussion subject.

Then follow the Annual Review & Renewal process discussing together. Once, you have completed the entire Annual Review & Renewal process, look at your vision and ensure it still fits. If not, revise it. Your vision is what furnishes the energy for you to continue to build the relationship you truly want.

ACKNOWLEDGMENTS

We have had the benefit of being partners and working on becoming increasingly better, and more fun, partners. We appreciate deeply the growth that writing this Workbook has produced in us and others.

Many friends helped us over the rough spots in our relationship. Sometimes, we were privileged to return the favor or to pass the favor on to others.

We have had much training and many work experiences allowing us to build our background in this subject.

We acknowledge and appreciate the couples who donated their time to test out the processes and questions in this Workbook. Their experiences fostered changes, additions, deletions, and corrections. They include Tracey Jo Duckworth, Sandy Dulaney, George Lester, Faith Lester, Joyce Lieher, Dave Small, Elaine Zumeta, and Jay Zumeta. In addition, several of our client couples tested the Annual Review & Renewal process as part of their work with us. They also provided comments to us.

Deborah Perdue at IlluminationGraphics.com was instrumental in creating the cover of this book, interior art, and publication coaching. We feel blessed by her skills.

We thank our editors:

> Our friend M. E. Steele-Pierce who found more items to adjust than we thought possible. Thank you.

> Our friend Kara Gall, www.karagall.com, who also is a writer and editor. She asks many great questions about how this relates to that. Sometimes we knew the answer. Thank you.

We acknowledge and appreciate the many teachers and coaches who teach us, allowing us to include some of their Energy Practices in this Workbook, and helped us develop new PEPs. These include:

> John Friedlander and Gloria Hemsher, authors of "Basic Psychic Development—A User's Guide to Auras, Chakras & Clairvoyance" plus other helpful books. www.psychicdevelopment.cc/

> Dennis Drake, RM/T, Shaman, 12 Strand Healer. Reiki Master/Teacher Medical Intuitive/Psychic Healer Psychic Instructor and Coach, Spiritual Mentor. Deceased

> Betty Miller, Licensed Massage Therapist, Van Wert, Ohio. Recently retired.

> Reverend Carol E. Parrish, Mystic, Author, Teacher, Counselor. Tahlequah, Oklahoma. www.caroleparrish.com

ABOUT THE AUTHORS

Reiki Masters Barb and Mort Nicholson have been married for fifty-three years. They complete the Annual Review & Renewal process outlined in this book once a year and hold a recommitment ceremony to honor their relationship about every ten years. Drawing upon years of experience in the fields of Social Work and Technical Management, they help their clients re-energize their personal and professional lives through belief coaching and personal energy practices. Please refer to www.nicholsonpep.com

Mort and Barb are both trained in many PEPs, which they share in individual sessions and classes with the intention that you learn to manage your own energy yourself!

As a retired Masters Social Worker and Reiki Master, Barb's specialty is personal energy work. She uses Reiki energy and consulting to help people heal and become the person they want to be. Refer to www.reiki.org/FAQ/FAQhomepage.html for more information regarding Reiki energy.

Mort, as a medical intuitive, helps people uncover and change their belief systems, that is, what they think is true for themselves. We all have many beliefs that serve us and our behavior flows easily and comfortably from them. Mort helps people identify which beliefs result in behaviors that keep them from achieving goals or feeling better about themselves, and then, with the person's permission, adjusting the underlying beliefs to different beliefs, a "rebelief," that serves and easily and comfortably supports the desired behavior. This new behavior has led many to personal and business success.

Our Mission:

Joyfully teach and model conscious use of personal energy in our lives. We are part of people taking their lives in new directions, gaining new perceptions and points of view, and achieving the results they want.

Web Based Information:

Visit our website : www.NicholsonPEP.com

Information regarding our work is also available on social media on LinkedIn and Facebook.

SAMPLE FORMS

NOTE: The following sample forms are included for your convenience. Please modify them as needed for your situation.

Please visit our book webpage

www.nicholsonpep.com/buildingrelationship

to obtain blank sample forms in full size.

EXAMPLE
Net Worth (date)

Asset	Value
Cash and Bank Accounts	
Partner 1 Checking	
Partner 2 Checking	
Common Checking	
Cash	
Savings	
Other	
Total Cash and Bank Accounts	
Other Assets	
House (Sales Price, rather than purchase price)	
Furniture, clothing, etc. (Sale Price)	
Car 1	
Car 2	
Boat	
Partner 1 Life Insurance cash value	
Jewelry (Sale Price)	
Total Other Assets	
Investments	
Partner 1 IRA	

Partner 2 IRA	
Stock from Partner 1's Grandpa	
Other stock	
Partner 2's Grandma's coin collection	
Total Investments	
Total Assets	
Liabilities	
Credit Cards	
Visa	
American Express	
MasterCard	
Total Credit Cards	
Other Liabilities	
Car 1 loan	
House	
School Loan	
Total Other Liabilities	
Total Liabilities	
Net Worth	

Sample Budget or Spending Plan

Item	Jan	Feb	Ma	Apr	May	Jun	Jul	Au	Sep	Oct	No	De	T
Income:													
Wages													
Bonus													
Gifts													
Sales-artwork													
Or other items													
Expenses:													
Auto Fuel													
Auto Maint.													
Auto Registr.													
Bank Fees													
Clothing													
Donations													
Dining Out													
Fun Movies													
Fun Other													
Groceries													
Gifts													
Health & Insur													
Hlth, Car, House													
Copays													

Sample Budget or Spending Plan

m	Jan	Feb	Ma	Apr	May	Jun	Jul	Au	Sep	Oct	No	De	Total
come:													
lasses													
eterinarian													
ouse: Maint													
Other													
iscellaneous													
Christmas													
Dry eaning													
emberships													
Haircuts													
Unplanned													
Other													
ersonal													
Golf													
Tennis													
ayments													
House													
Car													
rojects													
tilities													
ard													

Each Partner's Household Contributions
and Primary Responsibility

Contribution			Both	Comments
Regular				*Partner may link to another who actually does the work*
Cards: Paper				Birthday, etc.
Cards: Electronic				
Cat Feeding				
Cooking Breakfast Lunch Dinner				Normally _____
Data Entry Financial Bank Items				
Dry Cleaning				
Grocery Shopping				
Gift wrapping/ mailing				
House cleaning				Link to Cleaner
House & Equip Maintenance				
Laundry				
Litter Boxes				
Organizational Filing				Each files own material
Pay Bills with Computer				

Pay Bills by Hand				
Sweeping porches				

Watering Plants and lawn
  Inside
  Outside				

Intermittent				
Fertilizing				
Financial Review				
Income Tax				
Insurance Claims				
Mowing				Neither—condo
Oil Changes				
Pruning				

Spraying
  By house
  Rest of yard and trees
				Use hand
				sprayer
				Neither-condo

Travel details				
Weeding				